Roast Chicken and other Gypsy Stories

European University Studies

Europäische Hochschulschriften

Publications Universitaires Européennes

Series XIX

Ethnology

Abt. B Ethnology

Série XIX Series XIX

Ethnologie, anthropologie culturelle et sociale

B/ethnologie-générale

Anthropology-Ethnology

Section B: Ethnology

Vol./Bd. 75

PETER LANG

Frankfurt am Main · Berlin · Bern · Bruxelles · New York · Oxford · Wien

Jelena Čvorović

Roast Chicken and other Gypsy Stories

Oral Narratives among Serbian Gypsies

PETER LANG
Internationaler Verlag der Wissenschaften

Bibliographic Information published by the Deutsche Nationalbibliothek
The Deutsche Nationalbibliothek lists this publication in the Deutsche Nationalbibliografie; detailed bibliographic data is available in the internet at http://dnb.d-nb.de.

In this book the author re-used material
from the following articles:

"A Gypsy, Butterfly, and Gadje:
Narrative as Instruction for Behaviour",
from Folklore (2008) vol. 119 no. 1.
Reprinted by permission of the publisher Taylor & Francis Ltd,
„http://www.informaworld.com"

"Losing a River:
The Social Significance of Gypsy Oral Tradition",
from Fabula, (2009), vol 50, no 1/2.
Reprinted by permission of the publisher Walter de Gruyter.

"Gypsies Drown In Shallow Water:
Oral Narratives among Mačva Gypsies",
from *Journal of Folklore Research* (2006) vol 43. no 2.
Reprinted by permission of the publisher Indiana University Press

ISSN 0721-3549
ISBN 978-3-631-60403-8

www.peterlang.de

Acknowledgments

Special thanks to David Chorn and the Institute of Ethnography, Serbian Academy of Sciences and Arts.

Gipsy gold does not chink and glitter, it gleams in the sun and neighs in the dark.
Attributed to the Claddagh Gypsies of Galway

For Gypsydancer

Contents

Introduction

Sas taj Sas: there once was, there was…

With these words Serbian Gurbeti Gypsies begin a story in their Romani language. This manuscript discusses the performance of narratives as adaptive cultural behaviors among Gypsies in Mačva county, western Serbia. Storytelling is a universal activity and may well be oldest of the arts (Brown 1991). It has always provided a vehicle for the expression of ideas, particularly in societies relying on oral tradition. Key Birket-Smith has even argued that anthropology originated with a group of tribes-people listening to one of its members tell stories about the strange customs of a neighboring tribe (Cruikshank 1992).

The title of this book is the name of one of the humorous Gypsy stories, favorite among many Gypsy informants. I have chosen it because this particular story, in its context, is a direct expression of the basic expectations between Gypsy men and women regarding sex and methods of food provisioning. The plot is simple: a young man has to provide food - a roast chicken - to win over a young woman's love and sexual services. Along the way, in order to be successful, he steals and they both cheat and lie to others - their families and outsiders. The plot describes not only negotiations between the sexes concerning the interwoven world of foodstuff provision, sex and marriage (Symons 1979), but also characterizes the Gypsy way of life: humor and validation of their own sometimes not very noble actions, with which they face life and its obstacles. "Women like meat" (Biesele 1993:1) or as the Gypsies say: "Not even a grandmother would give [it] for free!", describing not only what women and men want and what they do it to get it, but also the notion of "the give and take" by which their community is sustained (Biesele 1993:2) in relation to others.

Many Serbian Gypsies refer to themselves as "smoked Serbs", or just Serbs. Some tribes reject altogether their connections with the Roma/Gypsy people, identifying instead with the tribe/kin group to which they belong. Frequently, they use the European term *cigani* or *zigeuner* as an added element to the name of their kin group. Therefore, the English term "Gypsy" is used throughout this manuscript, except when the Roma refer to themselves as such.

Gypsy and non-Gypsy populations have lived side by side in Europe for centuries and the experience, all round, has been less than satisfying. Gypsies are found all over Europe, with substantial populations in central and eastern Europe. In spite of their longstanding presence in Europe, their integration into European society has been poor (Arayici 1998). They are one of the few ethnic groups which have never laid claim to territory. And, yet, Gypsy history is a story of exclusion and discrimination. Legend, still alive in the rural Balkan countries, has it that

Gypsies manufactured the nails that were used to crucify Christ, and/or that they stole the fourth nail, thus making the crucifixion more painful (Djordjević 1932). Gypsy-hunting and other such persecutions have occurred almost from the beginning of the Gypsy presence in Europe, with a peak in the World War II (Crowe 1996). During the World War II approximately 300,000—600,000 Gypsies were murdered in the Holocaust. Gypsy discrimination continues to this day. Persecution and discrimination is now carried out by governments, communities, and individuals - especially in Eastern Europe and increasingly so since the fall of communism (Erlanger 2000).

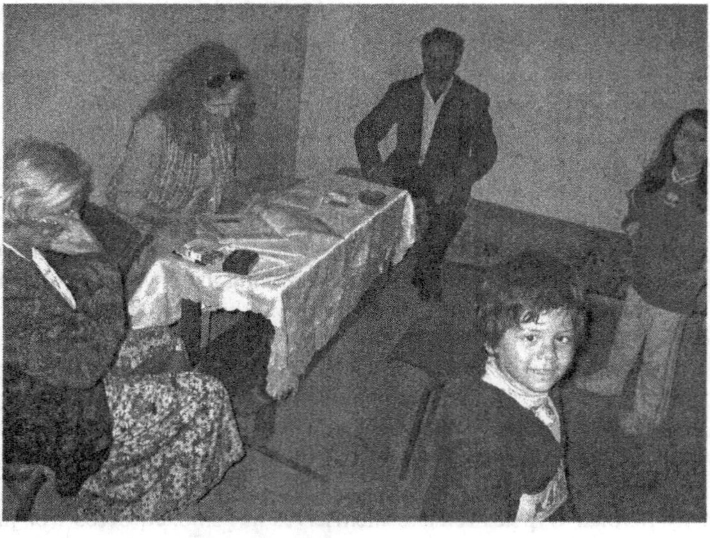

Literature on the Roma/Gypsies is vast and diverse, characterized by the absence of an empirical basis to most of the theorizing. Such a body of literature, especially one that emphasizes the exotic and isolated character of Gypsy culture, contributes still more to the present-day misconception of Gypsies and their behavior.

This book is based on the data collected during original fieldwork, carried out over several years (2002-2008), among rural Gypsies in Serbia. Mačva, a rural, agriculturally rich county in western Serbia, is a place where local Gypsy traditions are still alive and which help distinguish between Gypsy subgroups and the larger Serbian society. I first came to the Gypsy villages of Mačva in the spring of 2002. Data were collected on culturally prescribed behaviors as well as marital and reproductive histories from around 400 villagers in several selected villages of the Mačva area. Some of the examined traits include age distribution, education, socio-economic position, fertility, mortality, parental care, attitudes toward non-Gypsies and other Gypsy groups and several selected oral histories. During my fieldwork, genealogies, accurate as possible, were constructed as an important source of information. Many of the Mačva Gypsies, especially so the older ones, do not posses official birth certificates or other personal documents issued by the Serbian authorities. In this way, many of them are "hidden" from the officials and some of the important trends in their demography remain thus unrevealed. I interviewed informants from almost each household, especially elderly people, to obtain names, genealogical relationships, ages, current residences, and marital unions. Many did not know the exact dates - of their birth, or that of their children, or some other important events - but were mostly able to relate these to some external events or general time periods - a time after World War II, or during Tito's Yugoslavia, after the 1990's war, the Milošević's regime and so on. In spite of this general vagueness, most informants were sure about their exact kinship relationship to others in their village as well as the nature/history of the relationship. These smaller groups - kinship groups among these Gypsies - form the basis of social relationships and lasting social groups. The larger categories - such as ethnicity, country and even religion - are far less important in their daily lives.

Historical sources reveal that these Gypsies arrived in the Mačva villages in large kinship groups (Djordjević 1924). My genealogical study of Gypsies living in several Mačva villages has shown that closely bound and relatively separated kinship groups established residence in the villages over the last 150 years or so. The rural Gypsy populations usually have a "leader of the village" or representative, typically an established older male belonging to the largest descent group who can usually list more than half of the population as his relatives. These influential leaders were some of the first people to greet me, show me around and point out who "the best" storytellers in their villages were. And this is how I collected around 80 tales/traditional stories. The stories are part of a collection made from several different Gypsy groups exhibiting varying degrees of influence from Serbian culture. The stories were told in Serbian, recorded on the tape recorder and later translated into English. I have tried to stay as close to the original versions as possible, editing only for clarity and comprehensibility.

The theoretical approach used in this manuscript to address traditional stories represents part of a growing interest in the significance of story-telling in the evolution of Man. There exists a developed body of work that has examined literature as product of a psyche designed by natural selection: this approach uses knowledge and concepts of the evolutionary perspective to understand and explain characteristics of oral, literary creation and other forms of art (Carroll 1995, Storey

1996, Miller 2000, Pinker 1997). According to this approach, literature and its preceding oral representations should be seen as an extension of an individual's adaptive orientation to its environment, both social and natural. This approach is founded on four major principles derived from the evolutionary perspective: the relationship between an individual and his or her environment is a matrix concept which exists prior to all social, psychological and other concepts; the human mind has evolved through an adaptive process of natural selection; all proximate causes are regulated by the principles of inclusive fitness as ultimate cause; and all representation, including literary, is a form of cognitive mapping (Carroll 1995: 33, Carroll 2002:120-122). The matters of mate choice, mating strategies, female adultery, step-parenthood, cross-cultural patterns, motivation structure and narrative function have previously been examined by evolutionary psychologists, anthropologists and evolutionary-minded literary scholars (Daly and Wilson 1998, Scalise Sugiyama 2001, Scalise Sugiyama 1996, Gottschall et al. 2003, Gottschall et al. 2005, Boyd 1998, Boyd 2000, Storey 1996, Coe, Palmer, Aiken and Cassidy 2006, Steadman and Palmer 1997, Carroll 1999...).

While some of these evolutionary analyses focus on how stories reflect the evolved aspects of human nature, my approach is based on the assumption that narratives, like other forms of communication, can have an effect on behavior. Storytelling is species specific, occurs cross-culturally, and its content shows thematic uniformity across broadly different cultures. A general evolutionary prediction is that the oral tradition covers domains of information that were valuable to survival and reproduction (Scalise Sugiyama 2001, Coe, Palmer, Aiken and Cassidy 2006, Steadman and Palmer 1997). Narratives, thus, could serve as a means of passing on adaptively important knowledge and as models of behavior (Pinker 1997, Steadman and Palmer 1997, Scalise Sugiyama 2001).

Like many people around the world, Gypsies have used oral traditions as a source of knowledge and information on the history of their ancestors, proper kin behavior, economic life, relationships with other peoples, and many aspects of the everyday world. Also, like many people, Gypsies have told stories generation after generation and with relatively little alteration. The alterations that Gypsies have made in their traditional stories reflect their ability to adapt to local conditions and accommodate their own culture. In this way, their stories are analogous to Gypsy music in general, assimilated as it is from their surroundings and the native people present, and internalized within their own understanding (Bellman 1993). Like their extreme musical expressions, many of the Gypsy stories express "deep melancholy, heart-piercing grief, and wild despair" (Bellman 1998: 75). For the Serbian Gypsies, the stories provide identification with and understanding of characters' situation, feelings, and motives. In the absence of written documents, narratives and dramatic interactions involve the audience at an emotional level, promoting empathy and mnemotic device, for recalling content (Biesele 1993). At the same time, Gypsy stories combine instruction with pleasure, especially evident in their humorous stories, at a very gratifying and thus memorable level. The stories explore a range of successful social conduct, in specific situations - areas such as marriage, kin behavior and sharing and attitudes toward non-Gypsies - and the consequences of good or bad choices are described in many contexts. In fact, Gypsy stories illustrate how oral narratives can deal with universal adaptive problems, while simultaneously offering guides to overcoming these problems in new and unique social environments. And while the details of their stories may change, certain regular trends and challenges remain constant. That is to say, Gypsy stories are traditional stories in which particular elements, especially the main topic, stay unaltered and which are transmitted, in the form of cultural inheritance, from one generation of kin to the next (Coe, Palmer, Aiken and Cassidy 2006).

Also, like many other groups (MacDonald 1992), Gypsies have developed traditions that, at least for a time, served to keep them separate from surrounding peoples. In an attempt to interpret the social significance of Gypsy stories I have tried to relate the stories to Gypsy culture. To paraphrase Dundes, the ultimate goal should be to understand the human nature and not the nature of the oral literature as an end in itself (Dundes 1969: 421).

From the beginning, my fieldwork among the Mačva Gypsies relied heavily on close-up, personal experience and participation where possible, not just on observation. At the entry stage, I tried hard to build trust, aware all the time that I, as researcher-observer, too was being observed and evaluated. The Gypsy women I met turned out to be generous hosts and allies: they were constantly trying to feed me and my young daughter who often accompanied me to the Gypsy villages. The Gypsies were never paid for their services; instead, small gifts for children were presented - usually candies and sweets - and once this food sharing ritual had been established, I was permitted to share their life stories, everyday troubles and traditional narratives.

The ethnographic research I performed employed several kinds of data collection: interviews, filming, observation, and documenting.

As far as the collection of traditional stories, older members of the Gypsy community, especially women, turned out to be veritable treasurers of traditional Gypsy stories. Some narrators were better than others, but when we started to elucidate the stories and their meanings, most would often switch to events in their own life, trying to find within their own lives and behavior a connection with and application of the traditional narratives. In addition, most of the narrators disliked being interrupted, and the audience, including myself, duly respected that wish. Storytelling among Gypsies is a very social activity: the location at which the storytelling took place (the narrator's house or backyard) was always filled with people: family, kin, neighbors and children of all ages attended the event. Sometimes, the narrators would dismiss my questions as being unimportant to their own lives, or to Gypsy culture, and continued to tell the story at their own pace.

Finally, I made my research goals clear to the members of the Gypsy community and obtained their informed consent to the research beforehand. At the end of my fieldwork period, I offered my informants the chance to read the results of the research; but since most of them are illiterate or semi-literate, I ended up reading for hours to them about themselves and the things they have said. So, we laughed together, inspired by some event from their lives or the stories, or their usage of the characteristically black humor, and I realized it was actually the humor and a sense of the shared experience of living in Serbia that created the bond between us. In the end, we all came out with stories to remember and tell.

Throughout this manuscript, contemporary Gypsies are viewed through an anthropological lens with special emphasis on their storytelling as adaptive strategy. The storytelling tradition is presented using selected texts and explaining them in regard to their ethnography. All of the stories share common concepts and are presented in the order of preceding explanations assisting those of succeeding stories.

I Gypsy chronicle

"[former] Yugoslavia is the one and only country of true gourmands. In other countries, if you don't work, you don't have anything to eat, but in Yugoslavia, you can eat and drink and you don't have to work at all".

This is how a Gypsy from Mačva describes the joys of life in Serbia. Ever since their unexplained advent in Europe over nine centuries ago, the Gypsies have refused to fall in with conventional settled life (Fraser 1992). The Gypsies remain a people whose culture and customs are beleaguered with misinterpretation and who strongly adhere to their distinct traditions despite persistent social rejection and pressure to conform with the surrounding majorities.

Today, there are around 8-10 million Gypsies residing in Europe; geneticists best describe various Gypsy groups as a conglomerate of genetically isolated founder populations. Recent genetic research suggests that most Gypsies are genetically closer to Indians than to European populations (Kalaydjieva et al. 2001). More importantly, the research emphasizes the internal diversity of the Gypsies, who seem to be genetically far more heterogeneous than the autochthonous European populations.

The Gypsies are probably of northern Indian origin, having moved out of that area some time between 800 AD and 950 AD, migrating westwards towards Europe, and arriving there some time after 1100 AD (Hancock 1987). It is unclear as to why they left India, and there are no written explanatory documents. From linguistic influences preserved in all Romani dialects, it is most likely that the major Gypsy migration route traversed Persia, Armenia, Greece and the Slavic-speaking parts of the Balkans (Fraser 1992). A common legend about their origin is derived from an 11th century chronicle by a Persian historian, describing a group of 10,000-12,000 musicians and entertainers who were given as a gift to the ruler of Persia, Shah Bahram Gur, by an Indian Maharaja, during the 5th century (Vukanović 1983). Linguistic and historical data, supported by new genetic studies, suggest that the European Gypsies, encompassing a large number of socially different endogamous groups, may be a complex conglomerate of founder populations. Genetic results suggest a limited number of related initial founders, compatible with a small group of migrants splitting from a distinct caste or tribal group (Kalaydjieva et al. 2001). According to geneticists, during its subsequent history in Europe, this founder population divided into numerous socially separated and geographically dispersed endogamous groups; various historical records portray the wandering Gypsies as "a group of 30 to 100 people led by an elder". The divisions, regarded by geneticists as a likely "compound product of the ancestral tradition of the *jatis* of India", together with the new social environment - Gypsy slavery in Romania and oppressive legislation prohibiting Gypsies from most western European countries - can be considered as secondary bottlenecks, further reducing the number of unrelated founders in each group (Kalaydjieva et al. 1999).

The group/tribe is still the primary social unit of the Gypsies. Group/tribe identity and the consequent divisions, prescribed rules of behavior and endogamy, language and dialects, and religion are based on tradition. Within Europe, individual Gypsy groups can be divided into main metagroups: the Gypsies of East European extraction; the Sinti in Germany and Manouches in France and Catalonia; the Kaló in Spain, Ciganos in Portugal and Gitans of southern France; and the Romanichals of Britain (Fraser 1992). Out of these, the greatest variety is found in the Balkans, where many groups/tribes with distinct social boundaries exist (Marushiakova and Popov 1997). The various Gypsy groups/tribes or clans are usually called in Romani "*rromane endana*", or "*endaja*", depending on dialect.

In the Byzantine Empire, Gypsies constituted an oppressed caste and were regarded as Muslims (Tatars), intruders from the land occupied by the Muslims. Actually, the first record of Gypsies in Constantinople is from 1054; their first appearance in Europe came as military attachments to the Ottoman armies. Later, they were confused with members of the heretic sect of *Antiganoi,* meaning "untouchables". Upon their arrival in Europe, Gypsies were free to move around and work unmolested for a century or more before social and economic factors pushed them into a situation of enslavement (Hancock 1987). They were forbidden to enter churches or to intermarry with whites, and were permitted to follow only certain occupations. In fact, the Roma were the first people of color to immigrate in large numbers to Europe, and Europeans tended to treat them as outsiders.

Although demographic and historical data are limited, census data and tax registers suggest that the overall number of Gypsies in the Balkans in the 15th century was only about 17000 (Marushiakova and Popov 1997).

Today, the current size of the European Gypsy population is around 8 million and rising, equivalent to that of an average European country (Save the Children 2001). In terms of their absolute and relative size, the Gypsy population differs in both parts of Europe. Owing to the subjective nature of Gypsy ethnic identity and their "ethnic mimicry", their population figures should be treated as estimates. Only 1.5 million Gypsies live in the five largest Western European states, which have populations between 30 and 80 million each, and the rest of the Gypsy population resides in Central and Eastern Europe (Liegeois and Gheorghe 1995).

There are significant differences between the Gypsies of Western Europe and those of Central and Eastern Europe. Whereas Western European states generally tolerated traditional Gypsy practices, the policy of the then socialist governments in Central and Eastern Europe was to assimilate Gypsies and they were targeted for low-skilled employment within the centrally planned economy (Crowe 1996, Stewart 1997). Efforts were made to help Gypsies settle down and improve their economic and cultural position in the post-war years. A result of these efforts was the banning of nomadism in most of the countries in the region and the destruction of traditional Gypsy occupations. By the end of 1989, the totalitarian regimes in the Central and Eastern European socialist countries had collapsed heralding the beginning of the transition for most (Stokes 1993). Although there are differences among the countries in the timing, pace and intensity of the changes, some characteristics are common to all countries. The transition began at a time when the economies of these countries were close to collapse and when impoverishment and unemployment, especially among the gypsies, had risen significantly. The current position of Gypsies in Central and Eastern Europe mirrors that of their western European counterparts. Gypsies are perhaps the population group worst affected by unemployment in all countries of Central and Eastern Europe. They thus have high levels of unemployment, substandard housing, lack of education and skills and an increasing dependence on state benefits and services. Among the general Gypsy population in Europe, education and technology, for example, are not significant factors within the culture and are traditionally not considered important (Noncheva 2002). A notable example is their illiteracy: even when provided with a schooling system in their own language, many Gypsies fail to complete even a basic education (McDonald et al. 2001, Save the Children 2001). At the same time, their rate of criminality is high, although the maltreatment of Gypsies by judicial systems is as high (Ringold 2001). In the populations of post-communist states Gypsies number between 3 and 10%, and their birth-rate is more than twice the national averages (Erlanger 2000).

Gypsies in Serbia

The first written document referring to Gypsies in Serbia dates from 1348, when Stefan Dušan, Emperor of the Serbs and Greeks presented some Gypsy slaves to the monastery of Prizren, in Kosovo (Djordjević 1924). A large number of Gypsies may have come later to Serbia with the Turkish army after the 1300's. In Serbia, as in other South-Slavic countries areas under Turkish rule, Gypsies constituted a separate ethnic group: they lived apart in *mahalas*, in towns, or in isolated village areas, and had to pay special "gypsy" taxes to the Turks (Vukadinović 1983). In the Balkans, through the centuries of Turkish rule, Gypsy groups were segregated and strictly endogamous.

The classification of groups/tribes as such is not uniform all over Europe: in some areas, mainly in the former Yugoslavia, almost every single local Gypsy community assumes a specific name even when they do not display an evident difference in dialect and occupation (Djordjević 1932, Vukadinović 1983). In Serbia, Gypsies form a complex mixture of groups, within which one can identify a number of subgroups (Čvorović 2004). Most Gypsies do not regard themselves as members of a single cohesive group, but identify instead only with their subgroup. These subgroups may be distinguished by their occupation, language and religion; their religion often depending on their location and circumstances. Oftentimes, the names of the groups/tribes have been assigned by others rather than by the Gypsies themselves; sometimes, the names describe a characteristic trade, religious affiliation, or other geographical or historical reference, usually in a non-Gypsy language, hardly ever Romani. In the past, the extended family constituted the social unit of the Gypsies, and the occupational niches that they filled contributed to the Serbian economy. Even today, many Gypsies identify themselves by traditional occupations, even if such occupations are no longer in existence. The traditional occupations had made Gypsies a part of the economy, which benefited both themselves and non-Gypsies. The traditional Gypsy occupations included crafts such as trough-making, basket-weaving, spoon-making, blacksmithing, ironsmithing and musical entertainment. Today, although many of these traditional crafts are no longer in use, a Gypsy might still say: "I am…a coppersmith, a tinker, a basket-maker, a bear-leader…". Although the Gypsies made a contribution to the agriculturally based Serbian economy, they were despised by the Serbian peasantry; craftsmen in general were held in low esteem and always occupied an isolated and lowest status in the society (Djorjević 1932). In time, though, Gypsy artisan products became indispensable, especially in the Serbian lowland areas, where they could make a living by selling their crafts. In general, despite their antipathy towards the Gypsies, the Serbian peasantry displayed a lenient attitude towards them. They were never regarded as equals, but a general tolerance was evident: in rural areas, it was custom that every Serbian house provided alms

for Gypsies, justified by the belief that God had cursed the Gypsies and made beggars of them (Djordjević 1932:122). In everyday encounters, Gypsies were called craftsmen; blacksmiths were especially in demand, and there were frequent cases where these craftsmen were given land in a village in exchange for their services. In addition, partnerships in the trading of cattle were often forged with the local Serbian peasants. There was also a widespread belief that Gypsies bring good luck: if a Serb met a Gypsy in the morning, the day would be a good one since Gypsies only think in the present; if a Serb wanted his horses to be good, he should sleep with a female Gypsy and his horses would then gain the stamina and health of the Gypsy horses (Djordjević 1932:124). Nonetheless, in the Serbian folk tradition Gypsies were also considered to be unreliable: for instance, "the Gypsy empire lasted only three days". On the first day, the Gypsy emperor mounted his own mother and rode on her through a village; on the second day he hanged his own father, and on the third day he was dethroned (ibid, 125). Thus, for a short-enduring occurrence, Serbs still may say: "It lasts like the Gypsy empire".

Today, Gypsies live in all parts of Serbia. The largest number is in the South Morava Region (4.2 per cent of the total population) and the Niš Region (1.4 per cent of the total). In some municipalities of these two regions they account for as much as one third of the population: Surdulica, Bujanovac, Bojnik and Vladičin Han. These regions and municipalities are among the least developed in Serbia (Save the Children 2001). And while to some extent protected by the socialist regime, during the transition period it was the Gypsies who became the biggest losers (Čvorović 2004). At the same time, the Gypsies' demographic characteristics greatly differ from those of the population as a whole. Thus, they have high birth rates, death rates well above average and high infant mortality. The very high birth rate combined with relatively short life expectancy makes the Gypsies a very youthful population, made up of large families.

Owing to assimilation and manipulation of their own ethnicity, many Gypsies today deny their Gypsy ancestry. In the past, some intermarriage occurred between the Gypsies and Serbs, especially in places where Gypsies became fully assimilated with the local culture (Djordjević 1932). The incidence of intermarriage, however, was low and to this day Gypsies have remained a separate ethnic group. In spite of this, however, not all Gypsy people refer to themselves as Roma. Some prefer the term *cigani* (*zigeuner*). In addition, some European groups/ tribes of the Roma/Gypsies altogether reject the connection with the Roma people in general, for example the Sinti and Manouches (Mirga and Mruz 1997). This holds particularly true for the Roma/Gypsy ethnic/minority group in Serbia. Since their appearance in Europe, Gypsies have flirted with their ethnicity to the extent that many consider the Roma not to have an ethnic identity (Stewart 1997:28). The manipulation of their own ethnicity and origin is reflected in early sources. A number of early European historical accounts refer to the Gypsies as

Egyptians, and the term "Gypsy" is thought to mirror that assumption (Fraser 1992). According to these historical sources, the Gypsies themselves propagated the legend about their Egyptian origin; they represented themselves as dukes, kings and princes from Egypt. The inventive process of Gypsy traditions in Europe had begun: "In the entire chronicle of Gypsy history, the greatest trick of all was the one played on western Europe in the early 15th century" (ibid.:62). Gypsies/Roma had begun their sojourn in Europe by taking advantage of the Christian piety of the age. Since it was a Christian obligation to help pilgrims, especially the ones with documents of recommendation from rulers, the Gypsies created letters of passage from high government officials such as King Sigismund of Hungary, representing themselves as penitents for the sins of their ancestors who had rejected Christian teachings in Egypt. As a result of the sins of their ancestors, they were required to wander the earth as pilgrims seeking charity from others (Fraser 1992, Djordjević 1932).

A main characteristic of the Gypsy as ethnic group in Serbia is so-called "ethnic mimicry" or "favored identity", by which Gypsies declare themselves members of the majority community. According to the 1991 census, there were 140,237 Roma/Gypsy in Serbia, constituting 1.4% of the population. In the 2002 census, Gypsies numbered even less – 108,133. However, an official estimate of Serbia's true Gypsies ranges between 360,000 and 500,000, compared with 7,478,820. Serbs (Save the Children 2001).

Ethnicity issues are being discussed ardently among many Gypsies today. In 2002, they were granted the status of a national minority by the Serbian government. This legal act, however, did not affect Gypsy daily life or status. Some Gypsies are proud of their heritage, emphasizing that they have never "traded" their "gypsyness" for success in life. For instance, as the president of one local Gypsy association in the village of Mačvanski Pričinovići, in Mačva, commented:

> We just got the status of national minority from the officials. Some asked for it, and got it. I haven't. We were Gypsies/*cigani* before, now we are Roma. I don't care. I'm a Serbian *cigan* and Serbian *cigan* I will stay. But now we have the title: Roma.

Many others, though, still deny their Gypsy heritage, deferring instead to their "favored identity". This is evident from the following statement by a Karavlax Gypsy, from the village of Drenovac, also in Mačva:

> We were all born in Serbia: my great-grand father and his father, my father, and myself. My ancestors came from Romania, but I feel I belong here. We always behave like Serbs. I have never felt like a Gypsy, ever. We are all declared as Serbs, on all censuses. In this village, we don't speak Gypsy language. We speak Serbian, and we know some Romanian, but just a few phrases. We are not Roma, the others [people from other villages] are.

Even as of the present, Gypsies form a complex mixture of groups. In fact, there are a quite few subgroups of Gypsies in Serbia. Some of these have lost the Romani language and their mother tongue is Serbian. There are different forms of Romani depending on to which group the Gypsy belongs. Interaction between different groups is limited, and the form of spoken Romani is an important means of distinguishing between groups (Čvorović 2004). Furthermore, Gypsies have always come under several appellations and names. Each group represents a historical and, to a certain extent, localized entity. Gypsies have always depended on the needs and contacts with their host countries as a source of their livelihood; many times have Gypsies adopted their hosts' culture in response to the different requirements of their social and environmental surroundings. The result is a great diversity of Gypsy tribes and lack of identity as an integrated ethnic group. Therefore, Gypsy culture in general is extremely diverse and difficult to pinpoint. Their ethnicity is also a disputed and complex issue, stemming from the fact that most Gypsies do not regard themselves as members of a cohesive group, but identify instead with the subgroup to which they belong. Within these subgroups, language and religion also remain diverse; the religion which a Gypsy tribe or ethnic group might hold on to is dependent on location and circumstances. Until very recently, a custom common to all groups was that they did not mix with each other—there appeared to be a strongly emphasized antagonism among the groups. A system that divides these groups, much like a caste system, still exists in some parts of Serbia today. In the past, allowable marriage choices for the Gypsies were largely restricted to members of their own group. Females, in particular, were expected to marry someone within their own particular tribe - a rule that was closely adhered to.

A significant characteristic of Gypsies as a group is their adaptability to religious and political changes which reflect the current political climate. For example, some contemporary Christian Gypsies are ex-Muslims. Another example of Gypsy adaptability is the construction of new ethnic identities and new traditions. Among Gypsies, these new identities and traditions presume to restore an ancient origin, in spite of the complexity involved with the legality of, or even obvious contradictions to, the historical records. A notable example of invented tradition and change in the identity of the ethnic group usually called Gypsies is the emergence of the Egyptian community in Serbia and Kosovo. The invention of Roma/Egyptian/Ashkali ethnicity has been going on for a few decades, assuming various forms during this time, and anthropological interpretations and misinterpretations have compounded the contributions of other scholars, government officials and Roma themselves in the inventive process.

The Egyptians in various regions in the Balkans were, in fact, historically known under various names: Jedjupci, Gjupci, Egjup, Adjupci, or Jevg, for example (Djordjević 1932, Vukanović 1983)). These various appellations were used for Muslim Roma ethnic groups in Serbia, Kosovo, Macedonia and Montenegro. In

Montenegro, for example, these appellations are connected with their traditional occupations: they are also known as Kovači (Blacksmiths) or Ashkali (charcoal-burners) in Kosovo - occupations traditionally reserved for the Roma in the Balkans. With the passage of time, most of these local groups lost their Romani language and heritage, and adopted the language and customs of the surrounding majority.

The term "invented tradition" here includes traditions actually invented, constructed and formally instituted, emerging in a less traceable manner within a brief and datable period (Hobsbawm 1983). The whole process of publicly establishing a new identity for the Egyptians came to light in the 1970s; in the 1991 census for the former Yugoslavia, the Egyptians are mentioned and noted for the first time. The census data reveal there are around 6,355 Egyptians. However, according to the 1995 Egyptian internal census there were around 85,000 Egyptians in Kosovo (Zemon 2001). In 1999, just before the NATO bombing, and during the peace-talks in Rambouillet, an Egyptian named Abazi, a member of the Serbian delegation, argued:

> There are around 150,000 Egyptians in the Kosovo area today. We don't know the Romani language, but use only Albanian. Our children attend Albanian schools. We don't mix with other nations or with Roma. We don't celebrate Djurdjev-dan. Many centuries ago, the Turks moved us from Egypt to Kosovo (V. Nedeljković 2002).

Soon, the Egyptians had established themselves as a separate, though "imagined" community (Anderson 1996). Actually, the key element to their identity is the question of their ethno-genesis. Several scholars have joined efforts with those of the Egyptian leaders to draw up a definitive interpretation of historical documents which serve as testimony to the creation and development of this particular community (see S. Nedeljković 2003, Marashuikova et al. 2001, Zemon 2001, Courthiades 1999). The claimed connection to Egypt is allegedly substantiated by the historical data. As mentioned previously, the first Roma/Gypsies arriving in Western Europe in the early 15th century all claimed to be counts, dukes or even kings from "Little Egypt" and, therefore, their names, for example, Gitanos from the Greek Guftoi, were all derived from an Egyptian name (Djordjević 1932, Fraser 1992). This particular "Egyptian" legend is traced even as far as Moldon, where a hill near the western Greek town was called Gyppe, from the Egyptian, and was allegedly settled by the Gypsies/Roma. However, the region had always been known for its Roma settlements and never for "true" Egyptians who might have settled there under the Ottoman domination. Moreover, the Arabic language was never spoken in the Balkans (Laederich 2000). Nevertheless, folk stories about ancient Egypt persist till today in the oral traditions of even some Mačva Roma groups who are well aware of their origin.

Meanwhile, the quest to establish and maintain the Egyptians as a separate community took various forms. Various associations, parties and foundations were established for this purpose. Many of their recently established cultural associations and clubs bear the names "Pyramid", "Little Egypt", "Nefertiti" and so on (Zemon 2001). At the same time, various media have been created for the same purpose: magazine and journal publications, scientific and pseudo-scientific books attempt to establish and cement the Egyptians folklore and "ancient" history. In addition, many symbols relating to ancient Egypt, such as photographs of Pharaohs, Cleopatra or the pyramids, are displayed during gatherings as confirmation of their true identity (S. Nedeljković 2003). Despite these efforts, the Egyptian leaders and scholars still struggle to influence and convince the wider community, as well as the Egyptians themselves, that "...among this [Egyptians] ethnic community, there is an ethno-psychological self-confidence of belonging to a collective ethnic entity, different to other surrounding ethnicities...This [Egyptian] ethno-psychological self-confidence is taken to be...the most important "ethnic factor reflecting the distinctiveness of one community" (Zemon 2001: 66-67, my translation).

And, yet, while the Egyptian elite tries to distance itself from the Roma ethnic group, many of "the Egyptians" perceive themselves as Roma: they consider themselves to be Roma, they speak the Romani language, and some even participate actively in various Roma associations (S. Nedeljković 2003, P. Polansky 2003, personal communication). Some, on the other hand, declare themselves to be Albanians, Macedonians or Turks, depending on circumstances and the current political climate. In truth, the Egyptians speak the languages of the surrounding populations. In Kosovo, for instance, their native language is Albanian, but they use Romani and Turkish almost equally; in Macedonia and Serbia, they speak Albanian and Serbian. Furthermore, in spite of the allegedly encouraged endogamy, the Egyptians freely intermarry with other "ethnic" groups: in Kosovo, with the Roma and Ashkali (Laederich 2000, P. Polansky, p.c., May 2003).

Nonetheless, in spite of the efforts of the Egyptian elite, the ethnic identity of the Egyptians is still rather diminished and possessing of uncertain values and obligations. However, in time, and with sufficient repetition of invented traditional elements, political and media urging and encouraged endogamy, these elements may yet become "real" ethnic symbols for the Egyptians.

Following the Kosovo war, after the break up of the former Yugoslavia and the ceding of territory to the ethnic Albanians, yet a new minority emerged: the Ashkali. Many scholars identify the Ashkali group as Albanian-speaking Roma (P. Polansky, p.c., 2003, V. Nedeljković 2002, Vukanović 1983). In the past, the name "Ashkali" was used to denote the Roma ethnic group in southern Serbia and Kosovo; these were Muslim Gypsies who gradually had lost their Romani language and adopted the language and customs of the Albanian minority (Vukanović 1983:138). Their traditional occupations included blacksmithing and coppersmithing. Today, most Roma from Kosovo consider the Ashkali as well as the Egyptians to be Albanian-speaking Roma (P. Polansky, personal communication);

according to the Egyptians, the Ashkali are pure Egyptians who deliberately hid their identity, and the word "*ashkali*" comes from an Albanian word for charcoal (see also Marushiakova et. al 2001). Yet, following the Egyptian example, the Ashkali managed to found a political organization, by which they declared their separate ethnic identity. They claim that there are around 200,000 Ashkali in Serbia, of whom the majority were ejected from Kosovo after the war. The Ashkali in Serbia explicitly state that they are not Roma/Gypsies, nor Albanians, but a native people from Kosovo, having its own language that resembles only Albanian (V. Nedeljković 2001.). The Kosovo Ashkali, on the other hand, state that they came from Egypt; some of them therefore call themselves Hashkali, a name they claim was given to them by the Kosovo Roma. Today, they live in mostly Albanian villages, in their own *mahala* and follow mainly Albanian customs. In fact, most know their ancestors were Roma, but in their scramble to survive and avoid retaliation and discrimination against the Roma, the Ashkali now deny their Roma roots (P. Polansky, p.c.). In Kosovo, like the Roma themselves, they try to live without working, surviving on pensions and social assistance. The Ashkali community has produced several versions of their ethno-genesis and history, allegedly based on their oral traditions and folklore. The essential purpose of creating and inventing this new tradition was probably to distinguish themselves from other Roma and Egyptians. According to one legend, they came originally from Iran, arriving in the Balkans around the 4th century AD. The Askhali adopted the Illyrian language, while the Illyrians adopted the religion of the Ashkali themselves—Islam (Marushiakova et. al 2001). Another legend holds the Ashkali to be the colonists from ancient Rome, who came from Italy to Albania, which is why they speak the Albanian language. There is a third legend, too: the Ashkali originated in Askalon, in Biblical Palestine; therefore, the Ashkali originated in most ancient times and thus relate their name, civilization and culture to another Biblical nation.

The appearance of new communities among the Roma is on-going, and one cannot predict how many more will originate in the future. The emergence and existence of the present communities is unique inasmuch as external play has been involved in the "creation" of these new identities. In the former Yugoslavia the beginning of the transition period brought about ethnic competition and conflict that resulted in a decade of war; during the war and post-war years, a situation of general ethnic factionalism, the Egyptians and Ashkali revealed themselves. Before the Kosovo war, the Egyptians and Ashkali declared themselves mostly as Albanians. With the escalation of conflict between on one the side Serbia and Macedonia, and on the other, the ethnic Albanians, the Albanian speaking Roma emerged as two separate groups. The Serbian and Macedonian officials encouraged the creation and separation of these groups from the Albanian national minority: their emergence corresponded with their own political and national interests (S. Nedeljković 2003).

Many of the Roma leaders, however, resisted the emergence of the Egyptians and Ashkali, and actually see this phenomenon as a separatism that weakens the already loose unity of their national minority. One of the Roma leaders in Serbia, Dragan Vasiljković, president of the Roma Union of Western Serbia, argues:

> I take them [the Egyptians and Ashkali] to be Roma people. There is no proof that they originated in Egypt, or that they represent a different ethnic entity. What their leaders claim—is just a theory, without any historical evidence and connection. In fact, this is a calculated manipulation in order to avoid and deny their Roma roots, combined with the personal interests of their leaders. Just a decade ago, those same leaders were actively involved in our Roma movement, and today, they declare themselves to be a separate ethnic group - whether as Egyptians or Ashkali (personal communication, May 10, 2003).

The invention of tradition occurs more frequently when a rapid transformation of society weakens or destroys the social patterns for which "old" traditions had been designed (Hobsbawm 1983). The main problem for the groups concerned is the way the issue of invented tradition is represented and understood outside the anthropological discipline. Even when such invented traditions are revealed to be an intellectual ploy, the issue remains an emotional and political one for the peoples studied, particularly for those who are engaged in a struggle for political recognition. In the case of the Egyptians, it emerged within a few decades and established itself with great rapidity. The Egyptian newly-emerged "ethnic" tradition seeks to infuse certain values and norms of behavior by recurrence, which repeatedly implies continuity with the past and, thus, the ethnic group attempts to establish continuity with a suitable historic past. Their invented tradition serves to establish a social cohesion or the membership of a real or artificial group or a community. The instigators of such inventions are outsiders as well as insiders: anthropologists often participate in the creative process. However, the establishment and existence of such invented traditions also damages the hierarchy and unity among Roma.

The current trend of invention of Roma/Egyptians/Ashkali traditions is becoming ever more embedded into those cultures by way of people talking about them and practicing them. In Serbia, Gypsy culture itself is an issue in the struggle: "Inventions are common components in the ongoing development of authentic culture...invention is an ordinary event in the development of all discourse" (Hanson 1988:899). If we accept Clifford's (1988) standpoint that culture is an ongoing human creation, then, as in the case of the Serbian Roma, invention of traditions can be seen as the symbolic construction of social life.

In cross-cultural research, an "ethnic unit" or a cultunit is usually defined by language, political organization, and territorial contiguity (Abruzzi 1982:15). However, in Serbia various Gypsy groups are presently divided by language, absence of a common territorial abode and regional differences in their community organization. In Europe, most Gypsy/Roma tribes still heavily rely on the distinction between Roma and non-Roma, that is, *gadje* and non-*gadje* (Mirga and Mruz 1997). Central to this is the system of acceptable behavior for Gypsies and the notion of *marime*: drawing a distinction between behavior that is pure, *vujo*, and polluted, or *marime* (Hancock 1997). In the past, a violation of purity rules or any behavior disruptive to the Gypsy group resulted in expulsion from the group, or some form of punishment. A contact with *gadje*, especially a sexual one, was considered a kind of pollution. From an ecological perspective, an ethnic population/group is defined as an assemblage of individuals with a significant number of shared behavioral characteristics, a shared historical identity and a higher occurrence of marriage with members of the same population than with members of other populations (Abruzzi 1982:16). Among these, marriage is of central importance in the definition of ethnic populations: ethnic endogamy preserves the distinctive ethnic characteristics within a community. Ethnic endogamy thus functions as an isolating mechanism by enhancing ethnic identity and reproductive isolation of the population (van den Berghe 1979). Furthermore, ethnic endogamy also preserves and maintains the adaptive traits like reproductive and subsistence strategies, access to resources, or child-rearing practice. In contrast, intermarriage among different ethnic groups has a weakening effect upon differentiation within human communities and threatens to destroy traditions. Endogamy is often applied on a society-wide level and assists in setting of group boundaries (ibid.). Endogamy practices therefore assist to underline group identity and its uniqueness as against neighboring groups with whom marriages are discouraged.

In most European countries, including Serbia, the Gypsies remain a separate and distinctive ethnic group. Success in retaining their Gypsy group identity has been due to their refraining from intermarriage. In fact, throughout the Europe and especially in Eastern Europe, the Gypsy pattern of marriage has remained the same for centuries (Mirga and Mruz 1997). This pattern is characterized by an endogamous, early union/marriage, emphasis on the girls' virginity, and encouragement for all females to reproduce. This mode of behavior was acknowledged and encouraged by the Gypsy males in equal measure over the centuries. And although females play 'the subordinate" role to "dominant" males among Gypsies, there is always a demand and competition for women among Gypsies.

The formation of different Gypsy tribes/groups and their dispersal throughout Europe in the Middle Ages is explainable by the selection theory. When energetic demands for the efficient exploitation of different resources favor distinct adaptive strategies within the same environment, selection should produce socially diverse populations to the exclusion of one uniform (Wilson 2000, Abruzzi 1982). In certain environments, it may be energetically cheaper for distinct populations to exploit limited and non-overlapping sets of resources, than for one undifferentiated population to exploit the total range of available resources. The most common examples of this come from the anthropological literature on nomadic and sedentary populations (Barth 1969). Most significantly here is the differential demand for mobility. Overt competition has been reduced through the development of more or less symbiotic relations, imposed in part by the greater power of the dominant population. Nomadic pastorals and sedentary cultivators exhibit important symbiotic exchanges, yet they represent a significant degree of competition with each other as land, or a territory, is a finite resource required by both.

Since different strategies of resource exploitation select for different patterns of labor organization, selection within humans would favor any mechanism that maintained the adaptive organization of the community (Abruzzi 1982). Inasmuch as ethnic endogamy maintains local ethnic distinction, selection would specifically favor those mechanisms that reduced the incidence of intermarriage among different ethnic groups in communities where ethnic specialization occurs.

Under stable ecological conditions the number of independent isolating mechanisms separating two or more local ethnic groups should increase with time. Reproductive isolation underlies the recurring pattern of ethnic relations associated with expanding pioneer populations (Barth 1969). Initial flexible interactions evolve into more rigid, stereotypical exchanges as the number of immigrants increases and the competition over resources intensifies.

Premating mechanisms that foster "ethnic visibility" are quite common means used to enforce isolation between ethnic groups (Barth 1969, Abruzzi 1982). Such mechanisms limit the interaction of local populations and highlight the recognition of ethnic identity, reducing the likelihood of interethnic marriage. These premating mechanisms include residential concentration, occupations specific to or practiced predominantly by the group, distinct forms of dress and speech, prescribed patterns of social interaction, rules governing courtship and marriage and other factors that exhibit local ethnic distinctions. Since selection for ethnic differentiation operates upon learned behavioral patterns, the more such isolating mechanisms become institutionalized as part of the explicit rules of a community the greater is the likelihood that they will be maintained in that community in the following generations. The resulting stereotypes of behavior are likely to lead to socially adaptive, appropriate behaviors for a large portion of time (Wilson 2000, Daly and Wilson 1983).

Among Gypsies, it is possible that the division of the founder population into small groups/tribes occurred due to the pressure for higher mobility in the face of competition for resources and territory, and has been consolidated further by oppressive legislation and maltreatment, geographic dispersal and cultural and linguistic divergences.

The tribe/group, with its own endogamous professional-group organization, was for centuries the primary social unit of the Gypsies. Their ethnicity was maintained by rules governing tradition and endogamy, and their survival made possible by the reproductive strategies they employed (Čvorović 2004). Only very recent political and economic changes have led to Gypsies ceasing to practice their original professions, with a concomitant weakening of the traditional rules and endogamous practices.

Today, adherence to these behavioral rules varies from country to country, and in Serbia, from tribe to tribe. The storytelling tradition of Gypsies also appears to be influenced by societal changes. Their storytelling exhibits a traditionalism in conserving that which is important to their culture - in this sense, there are no new stories in their tradition, but, instead, additional invented retellings which incorporate the Gypsies new experiences. Over time, have Gypsy narrators have frequently changed the details of the stories and adapted them in relation to others; yet, still, certain regular motifs and challenges have remained constant.

II An overview of Gypsy Folklore in Mačva

Mačva is a rural, agriculturally rich county in western Serbia, inhabited by nearly 10,000 Gypsies whose local traditions are still alive and help distinguish between Gypsy subgroups and the larger Serbian society. Most of the Mačva Gypsies live, together with the Serbs, in fifty-two villages surrounding the county seat, Šabac.

Permanent occupancy of Mačva was first established by these Gypsies in the late nineteenth century; a second wave followed in the 1950's, when they were required to establish permanent residences by the Serbian government. This transition, from a nomadic to a more settled lifestyle did not, however, result in a complete breakdown of their traditions and former lifestyle.

The present Gypsy settlements are typically poor and often lacking in running water and sewage systems. Electrification in the area came relatively late, in the early 1970's, while roads connecting villages to each other and to Šabac are still rather rural. The majority of the Gypsy population in Mačva are semi-literate, and receive, on average, a little less than five-and-a-half years of regular schooling; they rarely engage in crop growing and farming, although some make a living as hired field workers on Serbian fields. Many are involved in trades of various sorts in the black/gray market economy. Typically, these Gypsies marry early and endogamously, and having a large number of children is seen as a form of social obligation. The extent of the kinship network is indeed influenced by the Gypsies' high fertility and vice versa: an abundance of assistance and services in the kinship group ensures a steady and high level of reproduction (Bereczkei 1998).

Usually, within a settlement, there are several kinship groups related to one another in some way, and this pattern is best described as a residential kinship group. Mačva Gypsies refer to these categories as their "nations". Groups of relatives within a village have numerous other relatives in other Mačva villages, and there is a lot of social activity between them. In every settlement at any one time, there are many temporary residents from other villages living with their relatives. This pattern of kinship residence is typical for Gypsies worldwide (Stewart 1997, Sutherland 1992). There are several Gypsy "nations" or subgroups living in Mačva today: the Kaldarasi, Karavlax (Romanian Gypsies), Čergari, Njamci, Gurbeti, and Horahane. Membership in a subgroup depends on descent alone, and given the traditional endogamy, the ancestry lineage includes descent through women as well as men.

Except for the Horahane, who are Muslims for the most part, all of these subgroups today are now Orthodox. In the past, distinctive occupations were usually passed down from father to son within each group. The different forms of Romani language spoken in these subgroups are an important means for distinguishing subgroup membership. Among the subgroups, a strong dislike is expressed and there is very little mutual cooperation.

On the social ladder, the Karavlax Gypsies rank at the top of the subgroups in Mačva, and they like to perceive themselves as more amiable and sophisticated than the others. This sophistication, as I am told by my informants, comes from the fact that they enjoy the best relationship with the Serbs in their village (Čvorović 2004). At the opposite extreme are the Čergari, until recently a wandering group, who occupy the lowest position and are tagged as a hostile, "tough, unpleasant people."

The Gypsy groups in Mačva have used oral traditions as a source of acquiring knowledge and information on the deeds of their ancestors, way of life, proper kin behavior, subsistence, social environment, relationships with non-Gypsies, and the everyday world (Čvorović 2006). Their traditional stories are presently still being transmitted, in the form of cultural inheritance, from one generation of kin to the next. In general, stories, like other forms of communication, can affect the behavior of an audience (Vaughn 1978), and some of these effects centre on survival and reproduction (Scalise Sugiyama 2001). Not all stories, however, have the same impact or function. For instance, there are several types of stories among Mačva Gypsies: some serve as entertainment only, such as their "scary" stories of the dead, humorous/funny stories and various jokes, and "educational" stories, of which the Gypsies, especially the older ones, refer to as their "school". In many instances, their stories are a mix of these types. All are enjoyed very much, especially the funny stories and jokes - there is a saying among the Karavlax Gypsies: "When are Gypsies happy? When we have roast chicken and stories to tell!"

In spite of village and economic differences, the Mačva Gypsies have characteristics in common: strong kinship ties, tribe/group endogamy and segregative attitudes and practices toward others, be it another Gypsy tribe or non-Gypsies. The main characteristic of their everyday life is extreme hospitality toward their kin and an active social life. Since most of these Gypsies are not employed or tied down daily jobs, they spend most of their time socializing. In addition to the "now and then" time they spend in subsistence economic activities, many Gypsies spend their time visiting relatives and just sitting around talking to each other and drinking Turkish coffee. The males, especially the older ones, gather daily to discuss daily village events, politics or sports. Older people of both genders engage in looking after their grandchildren, joking with and teasing children and the younger folk, while middle aged adults are busy with various tasks. Many Gypsy women, on the other hand, have turned afternoon coffee drinking into a daily ritual, a moment in time when they are free from their daily obligatory activities, such as cooking for their families and house cleaning. Usually, they gather in the backyard of each others houses, armed with pots of coffee, cigarettes and the latest gossip, along with their youngest children who cavort about freely. These children are rarely forbidden any form of entertainment activity. Older Gypsy women, "grandmothers" as they are all called regardless of their actual kin relation, turned out to be the true keepers of not only the small children but also of traditional stories, especially "the educational ones". This observation may, of course, have arisen from and been influenced by the fact, that as a female researcher, I had greater ready access to their "world" than that of their men. It is also documented, though, that among many people it is the mothers who tell the stories to the children (Coe, Palmer, Aiken, and Cassidy 2005). In almost every Gypsy settlement, men, I am told, prefer jokes and funny stories while women, when relating a story, prefer it to be more "as it should be", i.e., moving and exciting. Many times have I observed how one of the Gypsy "grandmothers" would gather children around her when they became too unbearable to tell them a story; often, it was also the case that the children would ask for a particular story they like. I have also heard younger Gypsies frequently referring to these stories as "old women's tales" and, even if they are able to tell the stories themselves, tend to defer to the older people when they are present (for similar experiences in many traditional societies see Biesele and Howell 1981, Narayan 1996).

Oftentimes, my recording of an informant's story turned into a "social action", exhibiting the transactional nature of the storytelling itself. Not only did I have to "share" stories or narratives from my own life in exchange for a story or life history, but also I had to "share" food and drinks and engage in "social" eating and drinking. Usually, Gypsy women would present "*meze*", a type of modest homemade bread appetizer, cheese and some tomatoes, depending on the season, while sometimes this would be a veritable feast with chicken wings or drumsticks and potatoes. Regardless of the village, food sharing among Gypsies is a social obligation - refusal to partake in eating and drinking and sharing whatever food there is would be taken as an offense by the hosts no matter how poor they appear to be.

The majority of Gypsy stories are a form of narrative which "puts chaotic events into an orderly form" (Coe, Aiken and Palmer 2006:25). At the end of the stories, "things make sense" (Jackson 1997:261) and the order returns to where Gypsies would like it to be. All of the stories tend to have a general structure, i.e., a beginning, middle and end, in which numerous problems appear that the characters attempt to solve or overcome. This is a cross-cultural feature (Scalise Sugiyama 2001b), the beginning establishing the setting and introducing the main character(s), the middle posing a problem or conflict while the end provides the resolution to the problem. Or, as Gypsies tend to say at the end of a story: "And so, that's the end: things return to where they should be". In many traditional cultures, it could take days or even years to hear a complete story, and one storytelling event might not expose the entire form (Coe, Aiken and Palmer 2006). In contrast, Gypsy stories are usually short and to the point, although a party/social gathering surrounding the event may take a whole day or night.

Gypsy traditional stories are either told in their entirety or in such a way that the point of the story, or the set of circumstances contextualizing a situation - for instance, the behavior it is designed to encourage, or that providing a theatrical cue, remains the same, regardless of the existence of various versions and structural changes over time. Unlike many other societies, where stories are not meant to be "taken literally" (Maynard-Smith 1984:14), the circumstances and devices used in most of the Gypsy stories provide indications that the story should be taken literally and directly. Gypsy storytellers often remember more or less precisely the entire story; details and descriptions (especially qualities attributed to a person such as the inter-usage of beautiful/nice/good, dark/black or big/important-wealthy, which may also come from Gypsy usage of Serbian language) may vary from teller to teller, but great emphasis is placed on the essence or the main theme of the story, both by the storyteller and the audience. Because Gypsy audiences often know the story beforehand, almost every mistake or straying from the central message is corrected. Once instance that I can recall, an elderly male informant got so upset with interruptions made by his wife, children and other relatives, that he had ordered them out of his house while he finished his narrative in his own pace and words. He complained that "they don't listen well" while his family tried to correct his words and the flow of events in the story ("It didn't happen like that but...", as if it were a true event and not a story), and he constantly switched to events and behaviors from his own life, there trying to find there a connection and application to the traditional narrative (Čvorović 2005), which in turn annoyed his family. His wife later commented that all he wants ("as always") is to attract attention to himself (see Miller 2000, Scalise Sugiyama 1996), and that he keeps talking [about "the old days"] even though there is no one to listen. In effect, inter-generational cooperation is essential for the traditional storytelling and for its transmission to the next generation – the story must be narrated and, more importantly, the others be must listening.

"The old days" and inter-generational mutual support are recurring themes among Gypsy elders in every settlement - almost every account and performance by the story-teller is colored by reminiscences of the past. Many Gypsies belonging to the older generation are troubled by the "modern" times and the present state of Gypsy affairs: their fading traditions, the loosening of morality and the lack of hierarchy where the old people "no longer restrain the young" while the young show ever-decreasing respect for the elderly. "The young [generation] is good for nothing", complained an old grandfather of four, "all they want is their damned cell phones. I had to trade a goat in Šabac [market place] to get my grandson one Nokia - and God knows why he wants one, we are out of reach [not covered by a local network] here anyway". I have heard many older Gypsies express a feeling of nostalgia for the "old days" when deference of young to old was greater. Not only do older Gypsies fear for fading customs such as storytelling and proper behavior, but there is also a sense of fear for their own personal position within a society. Some old Gypsies talk about themselves as being "of no use", referring not only to their dependent economic position (on their families, children and grandchildren) but also implying that old people these days no longer involve themselves in many village matters without considering the views of the younger generation.

As in many other cultures around the world, the primary storyteller within a family or extended family among the Gypsies is a parent or more likely a grandparent or close older kinsperson (Hallowell 2002, Calame-Griaule 1986, De Laguna 1997, Brown 1991). Among Gypsies, the elders generally tell the stories and when asked where they learned the story, informants usually said it was from a grandmother, grandfather or mother and less often from a father. Gypsy women often learned the stories from their mothers-in-law. In spite of their perception and sentiments on the fading traditions and influences of modern life, older people among Gypsies rarely become "useless" in everyday life and events, even if they have to depend economically on their children or grandchildren. As they age, they are still seen by their families and relatives as the "store-houses" of knowledge, both practical and traditional, accumulated over a lifetime. During my fieldwork, someone would say: "I'll take you to a grandmother/grandfather…; he/she's an old person and knows everything". In addition, old Gypsy people recognize from years of experience how best to maintain and balance their public life and kinship obligations within their communities. In many Gypsy settlements, kin ties to these older people are the basis for young people's initial social position within a settlement, and are especially important later on in marriage. In every Gypsy group with the exception of the Romanian Gypsies (Čvorović 2004), most marriages are still arranged within families, and who belongs to whom in terms of lineage of grandparents and the older generation plays a still significant role in these alliances. In everyday life, caring for small children, while their mothers are working around the house or elsewhere is another important function of older people, especially so for the older women. The pleasure these older people derive from knowing and repeating the traditional tales is apparent. They have heard these stories in all their numerous variations so often and for so long yet still enjoy telling the stories again to make new generations laugh and learn. From observation and interviews as well as from context in the performance of the stories, it is clear that many children and young people regard their grandparents as loving and educative.

To the extent that stories are retold generation after generation of close kin and have an effect on behavior, traditional stories might be best viewed as ancestral strategies that promote behavior that carried benefits for social fitness (Coe, Palmer, Aiken, and Cassidy 2005). Gypsy stories, then, can be best seen as providing each generation with rules of behavior, what ought to be done and in which way, and what ought not to be done (Hefner 1991:115). The ability to create and maintain social relationships, both within the nuclear and extended family as well within larger set of distant kin and non-kin, is crucial to the success of human descendancy and, hence, the most important of these rules are likely to be concerned with social behavior (Steadman and Palmer 1997:342). In fact, cooperation between close familial kin is also largely a product of parental encouragement - even altruism among close kin is transmitted culturally from one generation to the next. Social relationship and cooperation among people not recognized as actual kin or distant kin is often accompanied by metaphorical usage of close kin terms. Gypsy traditional stories by teaching – the substitution of potentially costly first-hand experience with verbal references thereto, i.e., relaying the consequences of social behavior, is a form of transmission of their social knowledge (Scalise Sugiyama 2001:221). Such knowledge is the basis of social cooperation. Many Gypsy stories use past events, actual or alleged, to anticipate future consequences, thereby influencing those who hear them to behave in certain ways.

Among Gypsies, storytelling is for most part the province of the elderly. I have suggested here that these traditional stories or parts thereof containing the intended "message" are consciously retold among Gypsies because of their particular influence on behavior. However, Coe, Aiken and Palmer (2006:22) have argued that "...parents do not tell stories to their children because they consciously want to influence them in ways that help the descendants. Indeed, ...[it] does not even imply that parents consciously want to influence their children in any manner whatsoever when telling them stories". Yet, not withstanding the arguments of Coe at al., above, I further suggest that storytelling of particular "educational" narratives among Gypsies presents a rationalized decision to tell stories with a specific content or point, in order to transmit basic values that guide social behavior. Many Gypsy traditional stories are situated in the context of their immediate social surroundings. Gypsy narrators deliberately choose one story over another, depending on audience and circumstances, altering at the same time the stories' content, to fit the local environment and serve their own needs. The function of myths and traditional stories is "to give moral and evaluative guidance" (Maynard Smith 1984:12), and these stories are repeated to influence others to behave in a particular manner (Malinowski 1931, Benjamin 1973, Steadman and Palmer 1997, Hefner 1991, Coe 2003). Gypsies are not unique in this: support comes from the ethnographic literature packed with traditional stories emphasizing the importance of appropriate social and moral behaviors (Basso 1990, Calame-Griaule 1986, Barongo 1997, Kuokkanen 1998, Elkin 1964, Middleton 1960, Coe, Palmer, Aiken and Cassidy 2005).

Storytelling among Gypsies is but just one of the numerous and entwined guides in their traditions used to influence the development and behavior of their children. In Serbia, Gypsies have developed complex traditional strategies that have helped them to cope with life's obstacles. For actions, rituals and rules of behavior repeated down the generations, Gypsies say "That's how our ancestors did it, so that's how we do it. It's good to do this way" (Djurić 1987: 253). Nevertheless, "...tradition works locally" (Arensberg 1937/1988:105). The Gypsies' pro-natal, endogamous tradition obviously has thus far helped them to survive and leave descendants, while retaining their group uniqueness at the same time. In

Serbia, kinship still remains an important basis for cooperation and a lot of what passes for ethnicity at the local level is actually kinship (Čvorović 2004). Hence, the Gypsy situation, characterized by segregation and low socio-economic status, could be partly self-imposed and a result of their traditional refusal to accept and become a part of the larger hierarchy of their host population.

In the following paragraphs, I consider narratives and interview quotes I collected in several Mačva villages and Gypsy settlements from members of a number of Gypsy subgroups, namely the Gurbeti, Čergari, Karavlax, Njamci and Horahane. These stories concern many aspects fundamental to Gypsy culture: finding and securing a mate, alleged ancestor practices, and relationships between Gypsies and other social groups both in the past and the present. The context of the stories and relationships between the characters represent various models of the Gypsy social environment and provide insights into the local consequences of a wide variety of actions.

As they were related, the stories spoke exclusively to Gypsy listeners about living as a Gypsy in a non-Gypsy world. The narrators chose to tell one story over another, their choice being based not only on my presence and recording of it ("I will now tell this story...because you have to know what is 'true' to Gypsies", "Please, grandma, not that story, it's stupid, tell the one that I like ..., it's better for us [our representation]"...) but also on the Gypsy audience. For instance, in almost every story of the "educational" type that I collected from Gypsy women, there were strong elements of a romantic love story, involving numerous obstacles and sufferings the lovers had to face, and the audience consisted of many "granddaughters", little girls, pre-teens and teenagers, a marriageable age in Gypsy culture. Scalise Sugiyama (1996) has argued that storytellers use narratives to manipulate an audience's representation of the social environment to serve their own social fitness ends, and this finding is not only consistent with storytelling in Gypsy culture but with other studies demonstrating social manipulation as integral to life and a recurring characteristic of the human evolutionary environment (Dunbar 1988). This social manipulation provides benefit to both parties: storyteller and audience. For example, when Gypsy "grandmothers" narrate a story about romantic and sexual involvement with a non-Gypsy, it serves as a warning of what might happen if one doesn't follow the Gypsy practice of endogamous marriage, while the audience safely gains the knowledge, through verbal representation, of the bad outcome of such behavior.

The ethnographic reality: Gypsy history begins with stories

During the course of my fieldwork among the Mačva Gypsies, I was able to stay and periodically revisit several villages where Gypsies reside and observe their daily life. Gone are the days of their wandering - the time they refer to as being "free as a bird"- these people have had a hard life and their hardship continues in the present. In a Gypsy settlement, daily life can be uneventful, the lazy pace interrupted only on certain occasions by village weddings, funerals or *slava*-(family holiday) days. Around the time when I first started to work in Gypsy Mačva villages, Gypsies were granted the status of national minority from the Serbian government. I was able thus to witness the changes brought about by this regulation and the sentiments it evoked, ranging from fear, hope or indifference. At that time, many Gypsies were unaware of their background, and local television as well as political leaders jointly informed them about their Indian origin. In one of my first stays among the Karavlax Gypsies in Drenovac, before these Gypsies accepted me as someone "just" interested in their stories and tradition, they mistook me for a government officer who they believed and feared was in their village to make a "list for India", that is, a passenger-ship list of all Gypsies declared as "Roma" for transfer back "home" to India. Many of them tried to assure me that "others are Roma, not us" and that they had no connection to the Roma people in the area. Soon, thereafter, they were given a free television channel which broadcasted programs in Romani language which these Gypsies didn't understand. In another settlement, the Njamci, many declared they are now Roma, expecting in return free medication: many lined up in a queue so that I could take their blood pressure and provide free medication. They thought of me as "a doctor without a white robe", and even after they learned that I am not *that* kind of doctor, many continued to ask for an aspirin, which in their opinion, is the "best" medication for everything, ranging from toothache to kidney problems. Others found it very amusing that in spite of all the "high" schools I had completed, I had ended up with them, in their dusty villages. In spite of their hardship and poverty, I for the most part experienced the majority of Gypsies as playful and humorous; even adults play games with children and adolescents and both men and women engage in sometimes vulgar joking and teasing. Their simple life philosophy is perhaps best expressed by the Gypsy saying: "Eat, drink and have fun and then shit on life!"

The Gurbeti Gypsies

The Gurbeti (their name coming from the Turkish for "beggar/wanderer") make up about two-thirds of the Gypsy population in Mačva. The tribe is part of a larger group known in Serbia as Arlije, or "settled Gypsies." In southern parts of Serbia, they are also known as Gadžikano Roma or "the ones who came (to Serbia) a long time ago" (Djordjević 1932). The Gurbeti in Mačva are relatively recent Orthodox Christians, most of them having converted from Islam about sixty to eighty years ago.

Approximately 500 Gurbeti Gypsies inhabit Mačvanski Pričinovići, a medium-sized, relatively wealthy village of about two thousand inhabitants, in many ways typical of Mačva's rural settlements. There are 750 houses, of which 110 belong to the Gurbeti Gypsy group. The majority of villagers are Serbs, whose main occupation is agriculture. Before the breakup of Yugoslavia, most Gypsies in this village were traders: they would travel to Bosnia, Croatia and Slovenia and sell cattle. Legal and illegal trade and smuggling of pigs, cows and chicken proved to be successful occupations at the time. Today, most of them are unemployed: during the summer season some occasionally work as fieldworkers, or do a black-market trade. During the winter, many males do not work at all; during the long winter nights, playing cards in a Gypsy "club" is a favorite activity, as is gambling for small sums of money. The Gypsies I interviewed like living in this village saying that "the richer the village, the richer the Gypsies," a reference to their relatively guaranteed seasonal jobs as field-workers in Serbian fields. The Gurbeti from this village like to declare themselves to be true Serbian Gypsies, and take great pride in the fact they have been residents of the same village for many years. All Gypsies in the village use Romani as their mother tongue. All of them also speak fluent Serbian, which little kids learn along with Romani in the early childhood. Their Romani language is a mixture of Romani and Serbian words. They assert that the only thing that distinguishes them from the Serbs is the color of their faces; in everything else—burial customs, diet, dress, and even language—they claim to be almost the same as the Serbs. However, unlike Serbian children from this village, very few Gypsy children are enrolled in public education. According to available estimates, around 30 Gypsy children are enrolled in a local school, which they attend more or less regularly. However, as pointed out by some Gypsy informants, most girls drop-out school at age 11-12, and get married. Most of the informants simply explained that they had learned "proper" behavior from their parents at home.

Almost every Gypsy subgroup in Mačva "owns" its own narrative about its particular founder and the origins of the subgroup. The Gurbeti still identify themselves as having an ancestor who was a blacksmith even though the demand for blacksmithing and the occupation itself have disappeared due to modernization. Today, the group chooses to preserve its identity by not mixing with other Gypsy subgroups in the area. Among these Gypsies, the basis of social organization is their kinship, which determines the hierarchy within the subgroup. The model of widespread cooperation within this particular Gypsy subgroup is the result of a hierarchical practice based on kinship behavior and the rites of personal recognition. A male informant in his 40s', Mika, expressed it this way:

> All tribes live by themselves: we don't mix with one another. One village, one tribe—that's the rule. I can always recognize my own. But others [Roma], they are very different from us; when I meet other Gypsies, I don't always get what they say, even though we speak the same language. That's because they have a very different mode of behavior and life than us. They used to go around in *čerga* [wagons]; I know we never did that, my father told me: we were never into *čerga*, begging and bears. We never marry them. We've

stayed ethnically pure because we've held on to our tradition and managed to maintain it and we still stick to it.

This cooperation increases the ability of the kinship groups to compete with outsiders, both other Gypsy groups and non-Gypsies. This is especially apparent when "doing business": during market days in Šabac, when Gypsies sell their products (cattle, crafts or items in demand on the black market, which Gypsies 'miraculously' manage to obtain first), the one who first arrives in the morning guards the available spaces for his co-villagers, mostly relatives of some or other kind, and chases off competitors from other subgroups (Čvorović 2006). The rivalry for the best spaces to display goods can occasionally manifest in a fistfight, in which case relatives within the subgroup come to the aid of the protagonist.

The Gurbeti particularly loathe Muslim Gypsies but also look down upon the area's other Gypsy subgroups. Muslim Gypsies are perceived as being entirely different. According to my informants, Muslim Gypsies "own no culture and no nothing." Even Orthodox Gypsies from other groups are envisioned as dissimilar and unrelated. An apparent distinction among Gypsies within this subgroup exists as well, based on how closely families or individuals preserve the old norms and distinctions. In this village, although Gypsies have largely adopted the behavior of the majority and dress, speak, and build houses like the Serbs, many have managed to effect a social separation not only from other Gypsy groups but from non-Gypsies as well. Even in relatively acculturated places such as this village, the "old ways" still account for much of the behavior.

Earlier, there was a sharp division between Gypsies and non-Gypsies in almost all aspects: clothes, life, marriage, food, cleaning, washing, etc. All non-Gypsies, i.e., Serbs, were considered *gadje*, in spite of generally amicable neighborly exchanges. Most of this is lost today except for the practices associated with marriage. It is expected, especially of females, to marry within their subgroup, and most follow this rule.

One elderly male informant informed me: "Gypsy history begins with stories", referring to the times when it was a kind of social responsibility to "sit around fire" and listen to traditional narratives. "This was when we didn't have electric power. What do you do on long winter nights? Sit with your family and have fun around a fireplace", this informant says. According to his words, every family "owned" a true, original story to tell, usually about one's ancestors and events that happened a long time ago. Some stories were about dragons, lost treasure, the Gypsy kingdom and fantastic creatures, while some stories addressed the immediate social environment – the relationship of Gypsies to "the others". After hearing several of the latter stories, it became clear that a sense of social difference is promoted in these traditional narratives, which usually warn of trouble if Gypsies become too involved with "the others." Today, their traditional stories are habitually still being told, despite the influences of modern-day life. Most of the younger informants stated that these stories are beautiful and "true to Gypsies", but they considered them passé, "old and conservative, characteristic of their grandparents time". However, as it turns out, most young people are very well aware of the contents of the frequently told stories, claiming they had learned it by heart at a younger age - because they were told them so many times. They would not, however, tell a story themselves, because "it's old peoples' business". One of the tribe's old stories cogently reveals the mode and essence of the Gypsy customs:

> Once, there was this Rom [man] who people used to call Bilc but his real name was Mihajlo. He worked as a craftsman, sometimes as a blacksmith. He worked in front of his own house, while his wife used to help him. Our women always help with our jobs—that's their duty. So, once, she went outside to help him; she was making underwear for him at the same time. She was supposed to be making "*turevina*", a special kind of male underwear that Muslims wear. It has one 'extra' part of textile on its back that sticks out. However, she didn't make it correctly, it being too small or too big for her man, so when he saw that, he became very angry. So angry was he that he hit his wife on her forehead with a hammer. She fell dead instantly. It wasn't his intention to kill his wife, but it happened. He got scared: what to do now, she's dead, her family lives in the same village, her kin will kill him. He started thinking, and arrived at a solution: he will drag her body into the house and wait for night to fall. He did as he thoughts dictated. When night fell his relatives came to visit. He told them everything, they were his kin, his blood, and naturally were willing to help. They conceived of a plan to take his dead wife to a nearby forest and bury her there. They covered her body with leaves. And that's how she remained - his dead wife. One day went by, another day went by, and another and another. Not being in her home, not showing her face, her relatives started to look for her: where is he, what's going on? A couple of children finally found her, buried under the pile of leaves: the children were biding their cattle in the forest, and immediately reported the dead body to the local policeman. Bilc was arrested; however, he couldn't be taken to the official [Serbian] court since he belonged to the Roma community. The Roma, however, never really gave the matter too much attention: It was his wife's family who were to decide what his punishment should be. At that time, the Roma had their own committee, *kris*, for judging and sentencing. *Kris* still exists among some Gypsies today. Then, his wife's brothers and his own brothers came to an agreement on his punishment: Bilc was to climb up a certain high tree, to the top, cross his legs there and light up a cigarette. Should he fall, he is done with his life—they will kill him; if he does not fall, he will be forgiven. In the event, Bilc

> made it: he climbed to the top of the tree, crossed his legs, lit up a cigarette and did not fall down. Everything was forgiven. This is a true story. It's how the laws were drafted among the Roma: to climb and cross legs without falling down. My grandmother told me this story; actually, this fellow Mihajlo is a cross-cousin of mine, but this story has been transmitted through the generations in my family, and that's how I learned about it. Until modernization [electric power] came, we would sit around the fire and tell stories. We have no history [written records] other than this - at home.

In cases of intra-group disputes, each Gypsy group determines its own form of mediation. In the past, each settlement was ruled by a chief, a man chosen for his age, experience, and wisdom (Crowe 1996, Fraser 1992). Within Serbian Gypsy settlements today, such men are called "representatives". To some extent, they are able to read and write. Usually, they settle minor disputes and the decisions are followed by the other members of the settlements. Formerly, if the matter to be settled was a serious one, such as theft, adultery, acts of physical violence, or complicated disputes between two parties, an honor court was summoned. This court is called the *kris*. The Gypsy "court"/*kris* is made up of committee of mostly older, respected, and established males, who judge "right or wrong" in cases of socially disruptive behavior and seek to reconcile the opposing sides. Thus, the honor court or *Kris* had decided on punishments and expulsions from the group. This court was the most important moral force in Gypsy life. Gypsy laws have never been written down or codified but have been passed for generations down by word of mouth. According to my informants, many Gypsies have interpreted laws according to contemporary custom, which has led to a great degree of flexibility in the interpretation of the laws. Some laws were gradually revised according to the needs of the group. In former times, there was a shared feeling that the law was unquestionably defined and "true" and few ever challenged this notion (Sutherland 1986).

In addition to the old Gypsy customs, the practice of *kris* or Gypsy honor court, and emphasis on kinship support, the story related above refers also to the widespread symbol of a holy mountain found in many European and especially Romanian tales (Adascalitei 1999). The symbol of the mountain is associated in an appealing way with the tree. In many other European tales, the climbing of a high tree is comparable to climbing a similarly inaccessible mountain at the centre of the world in order to purify one's soul. Our Gypsy, Bilc, was thus able to purify his soul and repent his doings, and so was forgiven.

The Njamci Gypsies

Njamci groups live scattered all over Mačva, with a substantial portion living in the county capital, the town of Šabac. A rural settlement of Gornja Vranjska, 7 kilometers from Šabac is home to approximately 150 Gypsies (Čvorović 2009a). The general socio-economic condition of these Gypsies can be described as one of acute and extensive poverty typified by massive unemployment, poor education, inadequate health care and poor quality housing. For example, the majority of the Gornja Vranjska Gypsies averages around 4 years of schooling (Čvorović 2008). To date, only five males have started secondary education. The one success among these moved on to Šabac and, with the help of his relatives working abroad, opened a flower and candle shop in Austria. In a later interview, he revealed that his "success" stems from the fact that people leave bouquets of flowers on graves at the main Šabac cemetery, which he later retrieves and resells in his little shop. In contrast, most of the Gypsies in his native settlement scrimp to survive; many engage in a black-market economy, in trades of various sorts, their income depending on the season. Njamci tend to marry at an early age, while rates of marriage dissolution and remarriage are high, as is fertility. Most marriages are unregistered, facilitating frequent breakups. The Gypsies justify breakups by explaining that when entering into unions at early age (as in marriage) "anything is possible". When asked why they have so many children when they cannot support them, one male informant cynically argued: "Poor people always have time for making babies—we don't have anything else [a job] to do. When you do business with the poor, all you can get are fleas. That's why we are so poor, no one wants to do business with us". They tend to marry within their and other Njamci groups from the area; another village is close by, inhabited by the same group and marriages are frequent. A male informant, a father of three marriageable-age daughters, the oldest being only 15, argued:

> We don't give away our daughters. For me, it's better that she marries someone poor from this village than a man I don't know, or I don't know about his family. Here, I know everybody, who would help you or not. That's the most important [in marriage]. Another thing is, these others [Gypsies], they steal. We don't. You can't marry someone who has a different mindset than your own.

Like many other Gypsies in the area, the Njamci were Muslims in the past but have no recollection of when and why they converted. They perceive their origin as being foreign, claiming to have come from Russia to Serbia after 1917 Revolution. They are fluent in both Romani and Serbian.

The Njamci in Gornja Vranjska maintain that traditional stories are still told almost every day, especially to young children and teenagers, for whom they are an important part of their education. One informant stated: "We have nothing to leave to our children, we are so poor and unfortunate, but we have culture, our culture is in these stories - that's why we tell them". In fact, many of the children do not attend the local school regularly; even when they do, most girls drop out of school in their early teens and get married. For many older Gypsies, these stories were regarded as the only means of proper "education" in addition to copying the everyday lifestyle of the older members of their extended family. Both the young and old Gypsies take great pleasure in storytelling; usually, the stories are told by grandparents or older members of the extended family. However, if it should happen that a grandparent overlooks or ignores some finer points of a story, the youngsters immediately interject and fill in the gaps. The stories are usually told in their full content - even lascivious parts are told to young children, since, only then are the stories "true". The following story tells of two brothers vying for the wrong girl, and the consequences they suffered. The Gypsies say that children can learn from the story about proper and improper choices, kin and brotherly love.

Two brothers

Once upon a time, two Gypsy brothers lived by the Sava river. They were poor but managed a living doing occasional coppersmithing. It happened that the two brothers fell in love with the same girl. The girl was Ruža [Rose], daughter of a rich landlord named Jovan. She had everything: black hair, brown eyes, a nice dress and a wide smile. Her father maintained her well and she was his proud and joy. The two brothers, greatly seduced by the girl's beauty, decided to ask for her hand in marriage. They traveled the whole night and reached Jovan's house by dawn. The brothers knocked on the house windows, yelling: "Jovan, you rich man, get up our father, open your doors for us!" Jovan answered: "Good day to you, brothers, why are you here, what is it that you want from me in this early hour?" The older brother explained: "Listen, father Jovan, we are not here to eat at your table, to drink and get drunk from your wine, but we are here to propose to your daughter, the beauty Ruža. Your Ruža is more beautiful than a rose, she is more beautiful than any fairy or ancient wine." Jovan then called his precious daughter: "Get up my child, apple of my eye, here are two men to ask for your hand, whom will you marry?" The beauty answered: "I will marry the one who can swim across the Sava River at its widest part, and no one else." When the brothers heard the beauty's request, they decided to give it a try. Hand in hand, they approached the river banks, and hand in hand, they entered the muddy water. When they reached the middle of the river, the younger brother began to complain: "My dear brother, I don't think I can swim longer, please hold me, please help me, the shore is close, we were both raised by the same mother!" But, the older brother was tired too: "My dear brother, I cannot swim anymore either, I cannot go any further, I'm drowning too, come closer so we can kiss and say goodbye, this long river will get us both!" So, immersed in the long river the two brothers embraced each other, and in embrace disappeared under the water. At the same time, Ruža was dancing on the river bank, joyfully tapping her feet, while on the other bank stood the brothers' old mother, pulling out her hair in sorrow.

Many Gypsy stories focus on kin relationships. Kinship pervades all aspects of their social life and governs the rules and conventions of how people within a certain kin category ought to behave towards one another. Much of the behavior encouraged by the stories includes forms of kin obligations obtaining to life's various significant events or phases, such as marriage and dying, as evinced in the story above. The two Gypsy brothers had sought the wrong girl because her background was different to theirs (her father being a rich land-owner), making their choice an ill-judged and unattainable one from the start. Nonetheless, the brothers had persevered until the end – and drowned together. The above story highlights the moral obligations of an individual – in this case being a true brother. In effect and taken to its extreme, what is portrayed and encouraged in this story is pure altruism – giving of oneself without regard to reward or the benefits of recognition and need.

The Čergari Gypsies

The name Čergari is derived from the Turkish word *čerga* (tent). All Čergari tribes belong to the larger group of Roma Tzarantza ("Gypsy tent" in Romani), which implies that they are wanderers or nomads (Djordjević 1932). By keeping apart from non-Gypsy and other Gypsy groups in the area, these gypsies are regarded as having retained the most "gypsy" distinctiveness. The Čergari inhabit several villages in Mačva: Mišar, Zablaće, and Dumača (Čvorović 2006). They are fluent in Romani and Serbian. Highly nomadic in the past, their men worked as coppersmiths while many of their women engaged in fortune-telling, healing, and begging. For the past forty years they have lived more or less permanently in Mačva. Taking advantage of the turmoil surrounding the wars of the 1990's, many of the Čergari from Dumača made money during the period of Milošević's regime and sanctions through illegal trade of cattle and coffee with Bosnia. There are around twenty houses inhabited by this subgroup in Dumača with a total population of approximately eighty persons. Most of their houses are new, unusually big for a rural Serbian area, decorated with ornaments and sculptures, lions and eagles being the favorite. A swimming pool or fountain decorates several houses, in spite of the shortages of running water in the area. These Čergari declare themselves to be pure Roma and stress their subgroup background and nomadic way of life. The Čergari women still wear traditional Gypsy clothes - wide, long bright skirts and scarves - and both males and females are likely to flash gold chains and teeth. Because of their previous nomadic life and frequent travels to Bosnia, they consider themselves as "cosmopolitans." The Čergari derogatorily label other Gypsies in Mačva as "peasants," a term used by other Gypsies to identify the Serbs in reference to the perception that they are tied to their land. An elderly female informant told the following about her life:

> We had no house, no nothing. Not even shoes. My husband was a coppersmith and my father too, and his father. We would move from place to place, my mother and father and three kids, my two brothers and me, and we never had a house. We were always on the move and never stayed at one place. . . . We used to go around with our *čerga*, and be very proud in our nice *čerga*, in camps, with pillows... When we, my brothers and I got older, we helped with trough-making too. We all worked, for it was a difficult time for everybody. We didn't go to school at all; and anyway, things were different back then—we didn't need school to make troughs and sell them. We were just really good in making things with our own hands, which was enough for us to survive and live.

When doing "business", the Čergari prefer Bosnians or Serbs to other Gypsies as trading partners, because, as I was told, other Gypsies "are not true Roma." The Čergari are very proud that they were able to maintain the Romani *Krisgomaji*, or "honor court," an institution allegedly once present among all Gypsies. Even though its existence today is mostly ceremonial, special deference is still paid to its members and their respective families. Among this group, females are treated with special importance: older women are especially respected and called "mothers" or "grandmothers". These Gypsies take great pride in the beauty of their virgin daughters, which they exchange for substantial sums of money at marriage. They still keep the practice of bride-price, something that distinguishes them from the many other Gypsy groups in the region who have adopted the Serbian custom of dowry. The Čergari say, "give me your gold and I'll give you mine" when "purchasing" a virgin for marriage. One female informant explains:

> We still buy women, sometimes for a high price. Our tribe always asks for an honest girl, a virgin. No one would marry a Gurbet Gypsy, or someone from Korakana [Horahane], or Kanjara [Romanian Gypsy], for they are beggars and they don't marry. I'm rich: I have four daughters, they will take care of me when I get all old and worthless. And they are good girls too. I still have to marry my youngest one; many have asked her but so far none has enough, good enough for her.

These Gypsies perceive other groups without the custom of bride-price as being "improperly" married, or not married at all. But, the informants also implied that members of these other groups would not have enough gold anyway to pay for a Čergari girl. Any Čergari girl who marries a Serb peasant is called *neverna* (unfaithful). In the past, such an act was meted out the same the punishment by the *Krisgomaji* as marital infidelity: expulsion from the group.

These Gypsies have low levels of formal education with more than two-thirds of them not completing elementary school. A male informant stated:

> I have five children together with my wife. None of my kids went to school, but they are doing just fine; they were never employed, but have worked for themselves; they messed around somewhat, and managed.

For many of these Gypsies, formal schooling was a substitute for "learning" through everyday life watching and copying their parents and older members of their extended family. Traditional stories are still narrated although not as much as in the past, and the majority of parents describe the effort in trying to teach their children about the history and practices of their ancestors. Elderly informants like to explain the Čergari's fondness toward nomadic life by quoting the alleged curse of a great magician who spoke these words to Čen, their ancestor: "You will wonder all through the Earth forever, you will never sleep at the same place, nor you will drink water from the same spring twice." As the father of five illiterate, now middle-aged children stated: "Many children will listen, the ones that want to know something; many will not." This following story about paradise is said to be "among" this tribe for generations:

> Gypsy Heaven
>
> Gypsy Heaven is one nice place to be! If only Gypsies were to know what great things await them - there are green fields, many sunflowers, fat horses running around and cornfields too. Also, there is a lot of food that we like: chickens, fish, cows and potatoes, as Gypsies can eat as much as they like to fill their stomachs until they're sick. Eat, drink and have fun, this God who made this, he must have had some Gypsy blood, when he has given us such pleasures. Also, this Heaven is covered with cheeses and sausages, and cheese is big as a house. And while all Gypsies eat and drink, *gadje* are outside, they see nothing of these beauties and they are hungry and beg for food. Gypsies laugh at them and give them nothing but scorn, not a bite of food. In this Heaven Gypsies sing, they sing loud and free, just like in this world, but in Heaven they sing happy, merry songs, nothing sad or blue like in this world. And the *gadje* cry, but not so Gypsies in this Heaven.

This story is probably inspired by the Gypsy's general feeling of powerlessness and the treatment they received from "others", as well as their actual hunger. A similar but more elaborate version of this story was collected among Bosnian Gypsies in the 1940's, with a clearer reference to *gadje*/the others (Tong 1989:163).

The Horahane Gypsies

The Horahane (or Xoroxane), a Muslim group of Gypsies, arrived in Serbia during the fourteenth and fifteenth centuries, accompanying the Turkish army. They are also known as Koran Gypsies, referring to their religious affiliation. The first written document referring to the Gypsies in Šabac, the main town in Mačva, dates from 1853 (Serbian State Archives). Since the end of Turkish rule, these Gypsies have lived segregated in the Šabac *mahala*, a Gypsy settlement at the outskirt of the town. Today, approximately 1200 Gypsies live in *the mahala* (Čvo-

rović 2006). In the past, their traditional occupations were ironsmithing, *dzambasluk* (horse training and trading), and musical entertainment. Some refer to themselves as "Egyptians", emphasizing their "different" background to other Gypsies and pointing out similarities in physical appearance: "I am the spitting image of an Egyptian, we are all elegant and small in posture, and dark skinned, and we also used to wear turban but not anymore!", laughingly explained a male informant. They, however, deny any connection with the Egyptian groups from Kosovo.

In their past, all members of this subgroup bore typically Turkish names; however during the wars of the 1990s in the former Yugoslavia, a substantial number converted to Orthodox Christianity and adopted new, Serbian names. The Horahane Gypsies in the Šabac *mahala* are fluent in Serbian while only few can speak Romani. They appear as the most diverse of the Gypsy groups/tribes. In their everyday life, they have incorporated many Islamic and Orthodox Christian elements: they bury their dead in the Turkish way, with a hodža (a religious scholar) reading the prayers, and celebrate the Islamic holidays of *Bajram* and *Ramazan* (Ramadan). At the same time they all celebrate Orthodox Christmas and *slava* (family/patron saint's day), a typical Serbian family holiday. I heard many informants claim they had to convert to Orthodoxy to "stay alive and in business" during the turmoil of the 1990's.

Presently, many of them are unemployed, though some have managed to open small repair shops where they also sell nails, hammers, and other tools. There are also several musical bands in the settlement that play at weddings, fairs and clubs. They are the most urban of all Gypsy groups. The majority of these Gypsies have adopted an urban lifestyle in dress and housing, and one can often hear them saying, proudly, "We are natives of Šabac". Economically, they are foremost among the Gypsy groups, owing to their residence in a town that offers many part-time and seasonal jobs. Recycling has only recently been introduced and many Gypsies see in this their chance for earning at least some money. In reality, their education and professional training falls well behind that of the neighboring Serbs, and their rate of state employment is low despite the presence of several elementary and high schools in the area, and also Zorka-Šabac, once the largest chemical factory in Serbia. One angry Gypsy told me:

> The non-Roma took over our traditional jobs: before, when Tito was alive, and in the past, it was the Roma who did the trade, crafts, black-market, fortune-telling, and music. Now, it is like we are expelled: nobody wants us, the non-Roma are doing our jobs, and that's why we are so poor.

These are, it turns out, typical of Gypsy sentiments in Serbia today (Čvorović 2004). Gypsies frequently mention Tito and "after the war [WW II] days", because, among other things, they were able to fully enjoy the fruits of Tito's communism: a guaranteed income despite there being little or no work at all, and the general enforced acceptance of all ethnic groups. The words of an elderly male informant, a once successful musician, typify the Gypsy attitude:

> I remember those days as my best. It was still Tito's time...Yugoslavia is gone forever, and there will never be a country like that. While Tito was alive... I could travel everywhere freely. I could have... smuggled whatever I wanted, coffee, or pigs, and have full pockets all the time. I could move around in Slovenia, Croatia, or among the Muslims and Hungarians, and all people were nice at that time. [former] Yugoslavia is the one and only country of gourmands... In other countries, if you don't work, you don't have anything to

eat, but in [former] Yugoslavia, you can eat and drink and don't have to work at all! That's why Yugoslavia is one rich, great country, where people enjoy life. In any other country in the world, if people would steal like they do here, that country would fail, but here, you don't even feel it...the more you steal here, the more there is to steal. I would never live anywhere else (Čvorović 2005).

As far as marriage practices go, a girl's virginity is obligatory for marriage. Like the other Gypsies in the area, these Gypsies usually marry within their settlement. If one of them marries a Gypsy from a different group, they label it as a "mixed marriage," while children from such a marriage are derogatorily called "mutts." Marriage ties with *gadje* (Serbs in this case) are virtually unknown. An unmarried, younger female informant explains: "[Serbs] don't want us, and then, that's not allowed. They have premarital sex, we don't, it's forbidden for us girls."

When asked to tell a story of his choice, an elderly informant sadly concluded: "There are many stories, all about Gypsy emperors and dragons. No one remembers them anymore. I grew up on these. My grandfather used to tell us, every day, about the Gypsy emperor and how things were in the past. But now, these modern kids, they make fun of me. They don't respect [the old ways] as we used to. Nevertheless, my grandkids know several of these stories. I taught them and hope they will teach their kids, too." Then he added: "There is a Gypsy saying: Gypsies drown even in shallow water... The way we are, if they [the younger generation] don't learn, it's goodbye [to Gypsy ways]". The following is a poem which he learned as a young boy:

I put a cradle under the plum tree
To put my child asleep
A rain will fall to bath my child,
A goat will come to feed my child,
There will be leaf to cover my child,
There will be wind to put my child asleep.

These lyrics epitomize in a very poetic sense the Gypsy philosophy of life. The poem captures the essence of the somewhat carefree Gypsy ways: there will always be some things in their immediate environment that they can use to fulfill existing needs without expending much effort on their part. Given their former lifestyle as frequent travelers and having being segregated and discriminated against, this practicality must have been true for their methods of making a living and, also, for childcare.

Many members of the older generation think nostalgically about the days of their grandfathers. They often describe the past in colorful terms, where Gypsies were a society of nomads - people who wandered the earth and never truly "had" anything but their freedom. In the past, their way of life meant that they traveled around the former Yugoslavia staying in different locations for various periods of time, in order to earn a living. This nomadism has been their way of life for many generations. Gypsies did what they knew in order to survive, and raise children along the way. This unstructured way of life - at least by conventional standards - is often discussed, with some melancholy: "When I was just a child, the best thing about this [Gypsy life] was, you wake up and you are free to go where ever you like – my family used to travel this way throughout [the former] Yugoslavia- everybody, my grandparents, little kids and babies, they all traveled from town to town, and there was not any supervision, we were free", explained an elderly Gypsy. In spite of the pleasant memories about their former lifestyle and liberties, there was a high price for the Gypsies to pay which they are still paying today: high infant and child mortality. In a recent study conducted among 222 Serbian Gypsy women, the infant mortality rate was almost 10%. (Čvorović, Rushton and Tenjević 2008). Reasons given by the women for the cause of death of their children were: 36.2% of the mothers claimed to not know the cause of death, while 36.2% claimed that their child/children were strangled by witches. Between 1971 and 1986 in the former Yugoslavia, Gypsy infants and children had a mortality rate more than three times that of the majority, viz., 0–1 years, 26.1 vs. 6.8%; 1–4 years, 3.3 vs. 1.0%; 5–9 years, 1.2 vs. 0.4% (Petrović 1992). A subsequent survey of around 7000 Gypsies found up to 50% of infants die before their second year, many cases due to accidents and neglect (Oxfam 2003). Overall, Gypsy hygiene is poor, little attention is paid to health, and there is resistance to child immunization programs (Čvorović 2004; Save the Children 2001). In addition to causes created by poverty, there are behavioral and cultural causes—lack of proper child care and investment, which contribute to the high mortality. In Gypsy culture, the father and other care-givers are valuable but mothers tend to be the most important caregivers so that their behavioral characteristics are without doubt the most important for child health. Among the general Gypsy population, a certain level of infant mortality is "expected" and, for some children, there may be an under-investment in care, feeding, and response to illnesses. For example, among one study group of Gypsy women (Čvorović et al. 2008), 73% of the deceased children were male, of which 21% were twins, implying perhaps, that Gypsies prefer and invest more in daughters as they have a greater chance of marrying up the socio-economic scale, and thus having more surviving grandchildren.

Many Gypsies seem to be aware of these facts: some openly joke on their own account about their untroubled attitudes towards children: "One day a little Gypsy boy fell into a septic tank; while the child was drowning, his father came by and saw what was happening. The father yelled to his wife: Hey, wife, should I save this one or we will make another one?" This, and other similar jokes told by Gypsies, frequently describe the seemingly careless attitude Gypsies have toward their own children. Furthermore, in the two above-mentioned studies (Čvorović et al. 2008, Oxfam 2003) all the Gypsy children died between ages 0-2, implying that the younger the child generally, the less impact the death seems to have. This may reveal an unconscious set of behaviors in the mother that reflects her culture and traditions. The neglect may be aided by cultural norms about child care—the loss of children is so common in the general Gypsy population that probably every woman grows up with the certain knowledge that she will lose children. For example, one of the mothers, a 47 year old Gypsy with 10 living children and 3 that had died, could not remember the cause of death of her children nor all the names of her living children or their year of birth. When asked why she has had so many children, she responded: "One for Death, one for me".

The Karavlax Gypsies

Karavlax Roma (black Vlax, or black Romanian) or Romanian Gypsies arrived in Serbia from Romania in the 18th and 19th centuries. They reside in several Mačva villages, the largest being the village of Drenovac. These Gypsies claim to be "natives" of Serbia, since, as they repeated constantly, their ancestors were born and raised in the same village, Drenovac (Čvorović 2004). They call themselves Lejaši, from the Romanian word *laiesi* (artisans). In the middle ages, the majority of Gypsies in Romania were slaves (Fraser 1992, Hancock 1987). The Gypsy slaves in Romania were divided into groups, serving either the Crown or noblemen or households. The *laiesi* represented the slave-group allowed to move about the estates doing a variety of jobs, including that of musicians. During their slavery, many of them escaped to Serbia, and after the abolition of slavery in 1864, migrated to Serbia in large numbers. They appear to have a somewhat darker skin color than the rest of the Gypsies, indicating perhaps, a larger degree of endogamy.

Ten percent of the 900 houses in Drenovac are inhabited by Gypsies. Almost all Gypsy houses are made of solid material, and furnished with modest but essential conveniences such as refrigerators, carpets and television sets. Romani, or Gypsy language is not spoken at all, while they are fluent in Serbian as their mother tongue and Romanian as a second language. They are all Orthodox Christians and celebrate *slava*, the ancient Serbian family holiday. Their traditional occupation was music: like their ancestors from Romania, most of them are musicians. The Gypsy musicians from Drenovac were famous for their virtuosity on instruments (Djordjević 1932). Unlike other Gypsy groups, they never worked as craftsmen, in demand in some places in impoverished 19th century Serbia. Then, the need for the products of the Gypsy craftsmen is what made such Gypsies acceptable in the villages. Musicians, however, were never needed in the agriculturally-based Serbian economy. And although their music was very highly rated, and they were the only ones to perform professionally, they could only occasionally make a living from their music, for example at weddings, village fairs and special occasions. They were paid in the form of a tip, making them dependant on the generosity and whim of the payers. Probably, in order to reduce potential conflict and encourage social relationships, the Lejaši worked out strategies to cooperate with the people in Drenovac. They made their own behavior acceptable to Serbs in the village by adopting the more stable, Serbian family life. Apparently, for the Lejaši, it was a calculated decision to become Serbs necessitating losing virtually all of their own traditions and their wider kinship ties to other Gypsies (Čvorović 2004). The fact that some Gypsies were in the village in the early 1700's (Šabac City Archives 25:46) suggests the possibility that one or a few thought up a way to get along with the Serbs, while others who followed may have been kinsmen who needed to accept the newly established rapprochement -- to the cost of their own Gypsy traditions.

In the past, the males from this group, as band musicians, traveled throughout the former Yugoslavia to play their music. These Gypsy musicians did not "read" music, allowing them more freedom to express its emotion. They picked up the music from their surroundings and adapted it to their own understanding (Djordjević 1932). Their music is imbued with a strong local character even though they are virtuosi at improvising.

Since the 1990's war, however, the majority of males have worked in a village factory, owned by a native Serb. The majority of females are housewives.

The Karavlax Gypsies perceive themselves as more refined than other Gypsy groups in the area; they rarely associate, whether in business or in social relationships, with other Gypsies. Instead, they claim to have managed to create lasting social relationships with the Serbs of their village; almost all have Serbian god-

parents. Kinship is very much treasured, as is the form of polite or "proper" address and behavior among kinsmen and with older people. They all bear Serbian traditional names. The custom of buying and selling of marriageable females does not exist among them. They consider themselves to be "true Serbs". A middle aged informant elaborated thus:

> My father, and his father, and my grand-grand father were all born in Serbia. They always behaved like Serbs. I'm the same way. I love my country very much. This is where I was born. I don't know where my ancestors came from, but I feel I belong here. Never in my life have I felt like a Gypsy, not even for a moment. I have the same soul [like the Serbs], the same blood, the same upbringing, the same everything. That's how I was raised.

Notwithstanding the fact that most of these Gypsies like to declare themselves as "true Serbs" many have begun over the past two years to publicly state they are now "true Roma", calling attention to their "ethnic revival" and pointing out the distinctiveness of their Roma/Gypsy culture (Čvorović 2009b). This ethnicity and attitude change was probably influenced by the general rise of nationalism in the present day Serbia and, perhaps more importantly, by the presence of several humanitarian organizations in the area which provide legal, humanitarian and material assistance to the Mačva Roma. Moreover, the relatively stable source of income for these Gypsies for years has ceased to be: the brick factory where the males used to work has been sold as part of the privatization process in the transition to a market economy. Hence, for the most Gypsies in the village, the only reliable source of income presently is the social and humanitarian assistance received. Thus, these "true Serbs", in order to become recipients of this assistance, decided to declare themselves as Roma/Gypsies. Some Gypsies with whom I spoke regarding this issue claimed they had to "convert" in order to survive, but others expressed relief because they finally see their chance to gain a "culture and identity" of their own. The fact that they are sponsored and paid by *gadje* in order to do so facilitates this process to a large degree.

Concerning traditional stories, my older informants, as in other Gypsy abodes, turned out to be true "treasurers" of folk tales and tradition. Since most of them are gifted musicians, their storytelling is often accompanied by an instrument, most often a violin, but also a guitar or harmonica. Several narrators were genuine performers, using music, acting and mimicry to point out or express some of the episodes in the narrated stories. The characteristic, black-humor was introduced at almost every turn during the storytelling, since, as Toma, an informant in his late 20s' and guitarist, explained: "...it's like with music, humor can alleviate just about anything. We do like stories very much, especially funny and sexy ones, they are enjoyed very much. It is fun for everybody, and it helps you to forget how we live". Toma's uncle, a middle aged retired musician, stated that Gypsies have to be like the Devil himself, using cunning and subversive strategies to survive, upon which he related this amusing story:

Once upon a time there was this great Gypsy king. He was tough and feared and all the rest of the Gypsy elders respected him very much. He was chief in everything. The Gypsy king used to drive around in his golden carriage, no one was equal to him, in his force and wealth. He was always accompanied by many followers, all Gypsies. The Gypsy king liked to take a nap after lunch, every day; if it happened to be a thunderstorm during his nap, Gypsies would start yelling: "Stop farting, you God, our king is sleeping!" Once, he gathered all the Gypsies to conquer the world. Where ever they appeared, they conquered everything and everybody. And then they reached the sea. The Gypsy king had a golden wand, and with this wand he parted the sea in two. With his army, he marched into the dry land between the parted sea. When the Gypsies reached half way along this dry path, the sea drew together again, swallowing all the Gypsies with the exception of one woman. This woman started to yell: "Ouch, I've lost the whole Gypsy tribe!" This was heard by the Devil, who suggested to this woman that they live as husband and wife. It is apparent that she accepted his offer because, look at Gypsies, black and devilish!

Although this story can be categorized as one relating Gypsy origins, it does not try to explain Gypsy origin, rather more, it attempt a justification of the Gypsies' position and stereotypes associated with Gypsy behavior in relation to their devilish attributes. Another amusing story, a favorite amongst my informants in this settlement, alludes to the relationship between Gypsies and Serbs. It is a variant of the story "The Church of Cheese", a recurring motif in Gypsy folklore (Djordjević 1932, Tong 1989).

How Gypsies ate the Church of Cheese

Once upon a time, the Serbs and Gypsies decided to build churches. The Serbs decided to build a church of cheese, because they had many cheeses and other food. The Gypsies had no food, so they decided to build a church out of pure stone. And that's what they did. After many days, both churches were built. And when the Serbs saw how nice the Gypsy church was, they wanted to trade with them: for their church of stone, Gypsies would get the church of cheese and some additional money as payment. And that's how it all happened, they exchanged churches but the Serbs never paid the Gypsies the promised money. The Gypsies were very hungry, and began to eat the church right away, with their many children. Little by little, the church disappeared; they had eaten it all up! And that is why the Gypsies have no church today. And that also is why the Gypsies are still asking for money [begging] from the Serbs, since the Serbs still owe them the money for the church! And that is why the Serbs have to give money to them!

This story is not only a self-justification for why Gypsies do not bow for any church (they have no firm "religion" or alter it to circumstance), but also rationalizes and justifies another Gypsy behavioral stereotype - begging. Again, Gypsies are portrayed as hungry and needy, willing to exchange just about anything for food (survival), while "the others" are made to appear as owing the Gypsies. In this way, asking for money or begging is self-validated.

Gypsy cultural stereotypes were probably formed by permanent discourse with the outside - their culture responding to non-Gypsy influences (Fraser 1992, Steward 1997). Gypsy culture responds in an ongoing dialogue with their social environment. However, Gypsies do not passively accept representations or models of behavior from their social network. They accept those that work, change those that do not and share and transmit those changes back into their social group in a continually evolving creative process (Di Maggio 1997). Together, these processes form an intertwined repository of factual knowledge about environment and attitudes toward the social world, supplementing education and continuing to influence behavior right up to the present.

III Selected tales and analysis

"We have nothing left from the olden times: our ancestors left us nothing but some stories, poverty and sorrow".

The stories presented here are by no means all that Mačva Gypsies are telling today. My own collection consists of around 80 stories of various types, collected among several Gypsy groups. The largest part belongs to humorous stories, "funny", so-called among Gypsies, which they enjoy very much. Then, there are the "educational" stories, which Gypsies refer to as "serious", but often their stories are a combination of these types. Indeed, many of these stories are not distinctive in terms of themes, and represent a local variant of a common story. Despite local variations in culture, and between the different religious and linguistic groups, there are many similarities in the narratives and tales among these Gypsy groups/tribes. In this chapter, I have chosen only a few stories to represent some of the main story groups. Apart from the fact that these stories illustrate and explore vital issues relevant for Gypsy survival and reproduction, such as marriage, residence, resources, tensions with the neighboring majority and proper modes of behavior, they also reflect cultural stereotypes and counter-stereotypes. In turn, these indicate the utility of the trait described for real-life communication and conduct. The stories rely heavily on typical essential features to remain recognizable and meaningful for the listeners.

The main groups represented in this chapter of tales are based on characters and themes, as follows:

1) Origin/ancestral stories
2) Love/marriage stories
3) Heroine stories
4) Humorous stories containing educational elements

All the story groups are effective in the sense that they appeal to the Gypsy audience with their recognizable motives and sentiments: they operate within the range of behaviors that are understandable and meaningful to the Gypsies (see Carroll 2001).

The other story groups, such as the scary/vampire stories and jokes, will be presented elsewhere.

The oral narratives are analyzed by relating the stories to Gypsy culture and behavior, that is, by giving special emphasis to those cultural behaviors of the characters in the stories that are encouraged and/or discouraged and which are presumed to have helped the Gypsy ancestors to survive and reproduce in the past. The emphasis will be on the stories that can be said to have a real and significant effect on social behavior - stories that function as "virtual reality" and enable acquisition of knowledge without undergoing the risks of first-hand experience.

Origin/ancestral stories

Almost every Gypsy group in Mačva has a distinctive narrative about its particular ancestor - the founder of the group - and about the origins of the group. These stories are not called "origin" stories by Gypsies who refer to them rather as "stories about us". Some Gypsies even claim that every kinship family has its "own" narrative and that nobody can tell a story that does not "belong" to their family group. The stories therefore provide Gypsies with a cultural identity and signal affiliation with a specific kinship group.

A Gurbeti family from Mačvanski Pričinovići with the last name of Jovanović, still remember having an ancestor who was a blacksmith. This storytelling event took place in front of a house belonging to Mika Jovanović, a "business" man who owns a small bar where many Gypsies gather daily. Several male members of his extended family were present, approving or complementing his account and vocabulary. Their colonization of Mačva is explained as follows:

> Our people came from India, that's what we are told. I don't know about it, what we know we heard from our old people. They say that three Gypsy brothers came to Mačvanski Pričinović. Three brothers, Marko, Jovanja and Joksim were blacksmiths. They traveled and moved around the world looking for a place to build a home. They carried their tools with them and stayed in places where people needed blacksmiths. They reached the village of Mačvanski Pričinovići. There were about three hundred Serbian houses and the brothers liked the village very much. They started blacksmithing there, and began our lineage. From the first brother, Marko, came the Marković family, from Jovanja the Jovanović family, and from Joksim the Joksimović family. We're all Marković, Jovanović or Joksimović in the village of Mačvanski Pričinovići. That's how we know who belongs to us: we're all kin, descended from one or other of the brothers. We used to be blacksmiths, but not any more.

In this particular tale, all three Gypsy brothers have typical Serbian first names, and they adopted the "ić" suffix, a feature denoting of Serbian origin. Many Gurbeti refer to themselves as the only true "Serbian" Gypsies, emphasizing at the same time the relatively good cooperation they have with "their" Serbs, having shared the same village for generations. Mutual economic benefit probably aided both these Gypsies and the Serbs, and the narrative encourages ethnic cooperation by playing down the Gypsies' foreign origins. Indeed, many of these Gypsies, especially the older ones, dislike the status recently accorded them - that of a separate national minority with an exotic, Indian origin. They are afraid it will jeopardize their relations and economic dealings with the Serbs in general, and many don't like to perceive themselves as being any different to the Serbs. An elderly informant, another Jovanović, explained:

> The Serbs here are the same as we are - equally uneducated, and in the same position. But now we have the title [Roma]. Not me. I am a Serbian *cigan* and will stay one permanently. I haven't asked for it [the "title"], and I don't think it would do any good to anybody, Serbs or Gypsies.

Yet another informant argued they needed rather a "good sewage system", instead of some Roma party, to unite them: "We have nothing in common with the others [other Gypsies]. Now, these Roma units create various parties, but they are not united, everybody loves to be a president, to be somebody. We now have two presidents in this village because people cannot get along with each other any more".

In addition, the ancestral story of these Gurbeti Gypsies confirms their distinctiveness from the other Gypsy groups in the area, by emphasizing kinship and past occupational specificity. A few years ago, my Gypsy informants told me, a young Gypsy man, known for his problematic behavior, provoked some trouble with several Serbs in the village. This man had been engaged in trade with several Serbian "hosts" ("good, honest people") and, according to my informants, behaved deceitfully which alienated the participating Serbs. In order to ease the tension, several "better off" Gypsies "bought" him off - gave him some money and sent him to live elsewhere. "He was a newcomer", explained Dragoslav Jovanović, "a distant relative from Bukor [a near by village] but really, good-for-nothing. That's how they are. After he was gone, everything settled down with our Serbs, we are good neighbors now, for they know us".

The Njamci Gypsies from Gornja Vranjska, quite unlike the Gurbeti, are keen to emphasize their "Russian" origin. The storytelling took place in November 2006, in a dilapidated little house owned by Mrs. Nikolić, an elderly female Gypsy, probably in her 70's (Čvorović 2009). Mrs. Nikolić believes that she is among the oldest ones in her settlement, taking great joy in the fact that, owing to her age, she can now do whatever she wants - she enjoys having visitors and a house "full of noise". She suffered a stroke recently, and her teeth are almost gone, but in her own words, that doesn't prevent her from telling stories to her great-grandchildren and grandchildren. The room was packed with her relatives including her eight grandchildren; she told the stories in fluent Serbian. During our first recording session, she chose to tell the story about the ancestor/founder of the group and the group's origin. This particular story has repeatedly been told in her family through the generations, and many of her grandchildren know it well. They refer to it as the "Lena story" which, in the Romani they use, means a river:

Our old people say "we are travelers." This story is what they say about the origin of our group, Njamci. Back in our homeland, India, we lost our fire. Our ancestors came out to look for the lost fire, and along the way, they lost a river, too. Actually, our old people say that the river moved away, and that is why we are on the move all the time: we look for our fire and river. The river they lost was Lena. It is only our group that calls every river Lena, other Gypsies do not have that word in their vocabulary.

Anyway, our ancestors searched and searched for the fire and the river, and they reached Russia in the 17th century. We never lived in one place, we moved and moved, and sometimes made camps near some river, but it was never the right one, so we had to move again. All old people talked about was the river Lena, all the time, everything centered around it - our everyday life, conversation, plans on how to find it. There were around 200 individuals in our group at that time. Sometimes they would all travel together, but most often they would split into several *čerga* [wagons] and travel individually, meeting at night at a chosen place. And every person had his or her own chores within the tribe. Our tribe would move and move, and then finally decide to camp for a while near some settlement.

Old women were fortune-tellers and healers. That is how they made money from local [non-Gypsy] people. Old women were also the primary care-givers of our children; they would gather plants to use them in healing ceremonies. Even today, we still have one magical plant that is used to stop

female [menstrual] bleeding; old women sell it in the local market, but I don't know if it really does anything. Before, all men were musicians, playing one instrument or another, and made their living by entertaining local people. There was one designated group of young girls who were dancers and served as a decoy for the local population [non-Gypsy]. They sold love to the local males, only to earn some money - they were, in fact, prostitutes. A girl like that would be really lucky if she conceived a child with a local man because he would sometimes provide some money or food for the child...Our little children worked their way through, too: they sold little things, like ribbons or baskets and made some money. That is still how most of our people live today: a Gypsy can sell a dead horse and trick a customer anytime!

In Russia, we were illiterate, and without an alphabet of course, but we used some special signs. These signs were in the form of engravings or little branches left along the way, usually by some river. For example, when one *čerga* needed to move along, they would leave these signs to the other *čerga* from the group. The signs explained whom of the local population they had antagonized so that the next *čerga* that came along didn't go to the same houses or people. This was done in order to prevent conflict with the locals; the signs were to point out who was swindled in the local population, how the locals received Gypsies, if the locals held any superstitions or were afraid of things like ghosts or vampires. This is how Gypsies make money from the locals - by petty crime, stealing, and fortune-telling. These signs conveyed the whole psychology of a settlement, and they certainly helped other Gypsies from the group.

In 1815, seven *čerga* had to flee from Russia, and they came to Serbia. This is how it happened: a young man named Nikola seduced and robbed one white local female, named Olga. She was a countess, or something. He was very handsome, and skillful, and had black hair like a raven's wing! Olga was also very beautiful and young, and they had a baby. So, the locals wanted to kill them all, but they managed to escape. Nikola's family escaped in seven wagons to Serbia, and they settled in Vranjska and Mačvanska Mitrovica. When they first got here, they claimed to be Russian princes and princesses, and they started doing everything: playing music, entertaining, trade of all kinds, until they got settled. They converted to Orthodoxy, to survive. That is why we have the same surname- Nikolić, from our ancestor Nikola who seduced the white Russian aristocrat. Two wagons later left to the Americas, the rest stayed here, and we are all relatives, the Nikolićs.

This story explains why these Gypsies acknowledge that they are Roma: Like many other Gypsies from the area, they perceive themselves culturally as different to the other groups from Mačva. Each generation, from the beginning to the end of this story, is taught to trace the origin of their group back to Russia and to an alleged ancestor named Nikola, and in this distinguish themselves from all other groups from the area. As one relative of Mrs. Nikolić puts it: "You hear these stories all the time, from our grandmothers to their children. Each tribe has its own, so we know who belongs to whom".

The broad, indistinct relationship between this ancestral story, Gypsy cultural practices and everyday reality is reflected by the fact that "Nikolić" is a common surname among non-Gypsies, i.e., the Serbs. The census for the Gornja Vranjska village discloses more than 20 Serbian families with this surname. In the late 19th century, after Serbia's liberation from the Turks, many Islamic Gypsies adopted Serbian last names (Djordjević 1932), a process which repeated itself during the 1990's, especially influenced by the war in Bosnia. These names indicate a Serbian ethnic identity, and their adoption, along with traditional Serbian customs and holidays, have helped Gypsies create trade relationships with the majority and become better accepted by them (Čvorović 2004). The representation in the story of origin of the Nikolić name reflects the effort by these Gypsies to adapt to the different requirements of their social surroundings as their ability to make a living has always been dependent upon interaction with their host populations.

The ancestral story also describes the typical Gypsy setting: Gypsies are traveling musicians and craftsmen who successfully use a range of behaviors involving stealing from, tricking, and manipulation of non-Gypsies. In the story, lying to, stealing from, and outwitting non-Gypsies are presented as socially accepted forms of behavior. In employing these behaviors, Gypsies have managed to survive, reproduce and maintain their separateness from the surrounding populations. These behaviors have indeed become the stereotypical traits of Gypsies. Shortly after their appearance in Europe, Gypsies obtained a reputation as thieves, fortune tellers and horse dealers of questionable honesty (Fraser 1992). To this day, Gypsies are generally associated with theft, lock-picking, purse-stealing, horse-thieving, casting of spells, and general witchcraft and trickery (Stewart 1997, Fraser 1992, MacDonald 2002). Throughout their history in Serbia, Gypsies have preferred only particular occupations in which they could be self-employed without having to acquire a formal education (Djordjević 1932, Čvorović 2006). With modernization, they have almost universally discarded old occupations in favor of new ones without compromising their freedom, ethnicity and residential flexibility (Fraser 1992). Various forms of misconduct, including stealing from and tricking *gadje* are still regarded as socially expected forms of behavior (Sutherland 1975). In the story, these behaviors are the basis of the entire relationship between Gypsies and non-Gypsies, and the manipulation of non-Gypsies is applauded. The story vindicates the stereotype: Gypsies rate highly an ability to obtain money, goods or food from the *gadje* by outwitting them.

The story of the first ancestor of the Karavlax Gypsies has many variants. One of the favorites, especially among the younger generation of musicians concerns "the dark wanderer". This narrative is distinct from the stories of similar type in form, style and performance. It is not narrated as are most Gypsy stories, but sung with the accompaniment of a guitar or some other instrument. It is the music and its performance that make it so appealing, according to the informant, a musician named Saša who performed this song for a recording. Presented in the form of a melancholic poem of monotonous tone with many romanticized representations, such rendition is explained by these Gypsies maintaining they are genuine "artists" (musicians) and not craftsmen like the rest of the Gypsy groups:

> The dark wanderer did not stop in front of the city gates. Riding bareback on his lazy mare he traveled around the world, he traveled around the world. He hasn't found gentler a God, or safer a tent. He traveled the world, around the world with his violin. The dark wanderer has lost his childhood. Without a beginning, he continuously searches for meaning and his background. Without a beginning he didn't have time to look back, to mark the road he has traveled, he has traveled around the world with his violin. No river has he crossed twice. He traveled the world, around the world, with his violin and lost the way back. Still he travels on his lazy horse, in a carriage with a broken wheel, around the world with his violin. He always runs away, runs away from ordinary life, from the boring grayness of one and the same countrysides. In his constant search for novelty, he never has found his real self, not his real self. He is shy and meek; rarely does he complain about the hardship of his life, the hardship, hardship of his life. He believes in apparitions. He is weak and cannot defend himself. [A lack of] defense would destroy many, but not him. He lives on, not by accident or luck. And God, God is constantly in his mouth. He says God when he hates and when he loves. He swears [at] God, angry at the indifference to his own. He never fought God, hungry most of the time, he did not eat his own church, not his own church. He fought life, and for a dream of some ancient existence, a dream of horses with wings, of horses with wings. In his dream, in the dream, he exchanges his lazy mare for a horse with wings. The horse with wings carries him along the roads of destiny, along the roads of destiny and around the world and brings him back to Serbia.

This song, explained my gifted informants, is usually sung at the end of a party or village gathering or *tezga* (a sponsored concert). "This song is a sad song, you don't want to drive away your audience before dawn", says Saša, who sings and plays a guitar in a local band. "This is a *fajront* [farewell] song". That would mean fewer tips for the band. We play this song often, here and when we play outside [the village]. This is our song, everybody knows about it. My father taught me how to play it, I think he learned it from his father. This grandfather of mine was a famous musician, he played in Šabac a lot. That's how we learn about music and songs".

Absence of the usual Gypsy representational form of this song points to the fact that these Gypsies have lost almost all of their once distinctive traditions (Čvorović 2004). Romani is not spoken at all; in fact, today only few individuals know several words. These Gypsies are the most acculturated Gypsies in the area and take great pride in this perception, as well as in the historical fact that their group arrived in Serbia from Romania already as Orthodox Christians, unlike so many other Gypsy groups that converted from Islam during the course of time or more recently. In the real life of these Gypsies, as in this song, a "gentle", Christian God is often mentioned; in the song, there is a clear allusion to acceptance of an unalterable religious affiliation. In the song, the Gypsy protagonist emphasizes true acceptance of the religion, even though he laments that this God has never accepted Gypsies and does nothing to prevent his people's misfortune. This could also be an allusion to the Serbs, the neighbors they share a God and nationality with (Čvorović 2004), but who have never truly accepted the Gypsies as equal partners, especially in marriage. In the absence of marriage kinship ties, these Romanian Gypsies emphasize instead their traditional godparenting with the Serbs, a cooperative relationship that has existed in their village for generations. Godparenting among the Serbs, a pre-Christian custom, is connected with the ancestral cult, and ties were formed between two families across generations. A godfather is considered to represent a mediator between living and dead kinsmen (Čajkanović 1973). In real life, the role of the godfather is of the greatest importance and he is a highly respected individual: traditionally a male, he names the newborn and does the baby's first hair-cutting; he also gives away the bride during a wedding ceremony and, in the past, mediated conflicts between families. In effect and according to Serbian customary law, godparents are treated like blood relatives; the Serbian Orthodox Church, too, has accepted and sanctioned this tie as a blood relationship (Milaš 1902:653, cited in Čajkanović 1973:275). Families connected by godparenting relationships are exogamous and said to be true kinsmen. Through these godparenting ties, the Gypsies and Serbs in the village have encouraged behavior which usually occurs between close relatives to also be directed toward non-kin. Thus, the most important effect of these kin-like ties among villagers of the Drenovac is that it has encouraged family-like cooperation between individuals of two very different ethnic groups. Godparenting ties with the Serbs is something that distinguishes these Gypsies from the rest in the area.

In this song, there is also a reference to another Gypsy story, the "Church of Cheese" but specifically denies Gypsy culpability or the "sin" of eating one's own church. Furthermore, the artist who created this particular song was also cognizant of another Gypsy stereotype - that of freedom, wandering and a liberated existence in spite of the encountered hardships. The Gypsy nomadic life style, lack of religious attachment, extreme musical articulation, and *laissez-faire* philosophy have been subjects of western literature and music over the past centuries to the present (Bellman 1998, Fraser 1992).

"This is how we used to live before coming here", explained Dušanka, once a singer, now a housewife; "all of it is true - Gypsies had nothing, just poking around. Yes, there were some horses and music and gaiety and all that gypsy business but no one could seriously live on that". "These songs are our folklore, nothing more, just like Americans have cowboys and Indians", explained Dragan, a male informant - "my ancestors were traveling musicians, that's how much I know".

In this song, a dream finally provides a tired Gypsy and his winged horse, a permanent resting place, in this case, a village in Serbia. In spite of their great emphasis on traditionally good relations with the Serbs, they were never regarded as equals, evident not only through their stories and songs but also through everyday behavior. For example, children of both ethnic groups play together frequently; however, one can discern a slight deference in the Gypsy children toward the Serbian children, especially so among boys. When playing football, for example, Serbian boys generally assume the role of the most famous football teams or players while the Gypsy boys have to contend with representing a losing team. Djokara, a 46 year old musician, laughs, and comments on this observation: "It's always the same. When I was young, we used to play cowboys and Indians [with the Serbs]. I was always the Indian, and had to surrender or die!"

The Horahane Gypsies ancestral story explains why the Roma celebrate the holiday of Djurdjevdan (Čvorović 2006). The following is a version of the Christian legend of Saint George, adapted and changed by this group to present it as a story of Gypsy origins. This version of the story was told by an elderly man knowledgeable, as he claimed, in Gypsy "business", stories and "everything else you are interested in".

> Once upon a time, many years ago, the Roma emperor ruled the empire of ancient Egypt. His empire was near a large and deep lake, and his people inhabited the areas around it. These were mostly Roma settlements. The lake was of crucial importance for the Roma: they used its water and for their cattle. One day, the emperor offended God: he cursed and swore at God and people the whole day, and prayed the whole night for forgiveness. Then a dreadful dragon was sent to live in the lake; and every day, in the twilight, the dragon would come out of the water and attack the Roma people. The animal killed many of them. The Roma were terrified and asked their emperor to help because the dragon killed and ate only the Roma people. The dragon would take a Roma child, or a woman, or a man, and it went on endlessly. The Roma emperor made a tough decision: to save his

people, he ordered that each and every house must give one of its members as a sacrifice to the terrible dragon. The Roma obeyed. And every household gave one child, one woman, one man, one brother, one father, as a sacrifice to the dragon. And that's how it was: the dragon would appear from the lake, take his victim and return to the lake until the next day. The people hoped that the dragon would leave them alone eventually. But the time had come for the emperor to offer his sacrifice: his precious daughter. The emperor couldn't bear it, and he ordered the army to fight the dragon. And the army came. Among many soldiers, there was Georgije [Serbian Djurdje], the greatest Gypsy warrior of all, and he killed the dragon after a long fight. After that, everything ended well, and the Roma decided to celebrate Djurdjevdan, in honor of the soldier Georgije who defeated the dragon. And this is what our old people would say: and we were there too, we ate and celebrated!

This particular group acknowledges that they are Gypsies but, unlike the other subgroups, their ancestral story implies that they could trace their origin to ancient Egypt. Gypsies have developed intricate adaptations in response to environmental, both social and natural, stimuli: as in many other things, Gypsies do not simply replicate familiar story elements but change and adapt them according to the current situation. A story such as the one above exemplifies this process. "Until modernization [electric power] came, we used to sit around the fire and tell stories. Roma history begins with stories", explained the informant who told the story (Čvorović 2006), stressing the great importance the stories had held in the past.

Earlier, most Gypsies had celebrated the so-called Gypsy holiday "Djurdjevdan", an altered version of an old Turkish folk holiday called *Erdeleze* or *Hidrellez*, dedicated to the coming of the new season or new year (Djordjević 1932:77). Nowadays, this holiday is celebrated on one of the Serb's *slava* dates. *Slava*, as already noted, are Patron Saint's Day celebrations. The Gypsy Djurdjevdan, in its initial form, was not linked to the *slava* ceremonies among the Serbs (Čajkanović 1924). Eventually, in time, under the influence of the dominant Serbian culture and with the conversion to Orthodoxy, Gypsies modified the character and function of the holiday, adapting it to fit their actual circumstances, both within the majority group and in relation to other Gypsy groups.

This and other similar stories, in which Gypsies have made changes to characters, functions and settings, reflect the changes that Gypsies made in everyday life and customs in order to create the most favorable strategy in a given environment. In real life, Gypsies justify the changes in their identity, names and religion as "inevitable" due to the dictates of the changing political or social environment. They often state they "had to" convert to another religion and change their names, behavior and customs in order to survive. In a way, the Gypsy custom of changing attitudes and identities reflects the current "mainstream" within Serbian society, since they always adopt the most popular, most widespread and most accepted option present at a given time. For instance, not very many Gypsies vote at elections, but of those that do, many frequently state that they always vote for the politician or party currently in power, regardless of their personal choice or the policies on offer. During the Milošević era (1990-2000), as I am told, every Gypsy that voted, voted in his favor, because he was seen by them as "the main guy"[the most influential]. After that period, and especially with the political changes occurring after October 5 2000, all of these Gypsies suddenly "converted" to favoring democracy and its representative at the time, Koštunica. "We all voted for Koštunica", says one male informant, because "he's the most popular now. We'll vote for someone else, when he gets into power". With this sycophantic attitude, they hope to gain whatever benefits they can get from the current government, regardless who or what it represents.

The "about us" stories can be classified as of the type of ancestral stories that contain "true speech" (Stewart 1997). That is, that these and similar stories "have to be true" because they have been learned from the ancestors and retold many times to the younger generations. By repeating the same story heard from the ancestors, whether true or not, these Gypsies create cooperative social behavior, a form of altruism within their own group, and transmit this culturally from one generation to the next. These stories are as much about the present and the future as they are about the past. The settings and characters are of bygone times but there is still much to carry into present thinking and to store up for future reference. These kinds of stories allow Gypsies to acquire knowledge with a device for identifying "who is who" in their current social world and instructions on how to behave accordingly. A social separation among categories of kin is very much encouraged, and there is little cooperation between them. Within each category, or "tribe," kinship is the basis for social involvement and hierarchy, and mutual aid and daily economic cooperation is expected between relatives (Čvorović 2006).

Love/marriage stories

Many Gypsy stories deal with marriage. A large proportion of these stories concern the process of attracting and securing marriageable partners. In the following story, collected among the Karavlax Gypsies, the main male character, a poor young Gypsy, is motivated to obtain not only a wife but also social status and material wealth by marriage:

> This event happened in some ancient times. There was a great emperor, who ruled many peoples. He had a very beautiful daughter, whom he adored. The emperor wanted to marry her off to the first among the best of all men: the strongest, the tallest, the richest. When the time was right, many suitors gathered from all over the empire. But none was good enough

for the emperor's daughter. So, the emperor made a decision: suitors will all compete, not with each other, but with cold weather. Their task was this: the suitor had to climb the highest mountain, in the middle of winter, naked, without any covers and not fall asleep. Many tried, but none succeeded. Then, one poor man appeared: he was a Gypsy, without anything or anybody, but who desperately wanted to marry the emperor's daughter. His problem was—he didn't know how to do it. The Gypsy would give his life just to marry the girl. He thought about it, and decided to go and see a wise man, well-known for his wisdom. So he did. The Gypsy came to see the wise man, and told him: "I want to marry the emperor's daughter. I'm poor and I'm sick of being poor and nobody. I want to have a wife who can finally make me happy". The wise man responded: "My friend, that's not a problem at all. How would you do it? Just you listen to me, that's how". The Gypsy exclaimed: "Dear God but how will I do it? Many of the best men in this empire have died on the mountain, from cold. How could I endure such weather, being so weak and malnourished?" The wise man said: "You just hang in there, listen to my advice, and you'll make it". The Gypsy agreed. "You say that the task is to climb the highest mountain, naked, with no covers, and that you must not fall asleep, or you'll die?" asked the wise man. "Here is what you'll do. You will make it, on the top of the mountain, naked, and you will not fall asleep. You will succeed where everybody else has failed. And here is why: I will light a huge fire at the foothill of the mountain, and I will keep it going all night long. You will look at the fire, and you will imagine that it is heating you, warming you up so you won't freeze. But, you must not fall asleep, not even for a second, otherwise you'll die like the rest" said the man. The Gypsy then went in front of the emperor, and told him that he is ready to go through all the trials, just to marry his daughter. Everybody laughed at him: look at him, he's a Gypsy, weak and poor, and he wants to marry the princess! The emperor allowed him to try, for he was certain that the Gypsy would not succeed. So, the Gypsy climbed the mountain, took off his dirty clothes, and stayed awake the whole night. He was looking at the fire, imagining that he was not cold, hungry or scared. And he succeeded. Just as the wise man had told him he would. And the emperor couldn't go back on his word: he had to give his daughter for the Gypsy. And so, in those ancient times, the poor Gypsy became happy and had many children. And this is what our ancestors would say: "And we were there too, we ate and celebrated!"

In this story, the poor Gypsy adopts a risky competitive strategy to obtain a wife, and with the help of a man with supernatural powers, he manages to do so. This is a variant of the common theme in folktales about marriage worldwide: males have to endure physical hardiness or risk in order to gain and secure a female

(Gottschall et al. 2003:375). After the Gypsy had been purified by climbing a mountain (Adascalite 1999), he passed the test, and was granted with a rich wife who bore him many children, a good reason for happiness for him and his fellow Gypsies.

The next story contains elements of a true but tragic love story: a beautiful young girl and her lover are unable to unite in marriage due to her family's disagreement. Even death could not unite them, leaving the girl's lover's spirit rummaging around for her.

Spooky Love

A long time ago, there was this good and beautiful young girl. She lived in this village with her family, mother, father and brothers. She was the only daughter, and her brothers took good care of her. The girl was beautiful, she had black hair and nice eyes. When it was about the right time for her to get married, she fell in love with a boy, also a Gypsy. But, her parents were against their love and forbade them to see each other. He was poor, and his family had a bad reputation, but she fell for him - that's how young people are. Next, there was a war: Gypsies also went to wars. And this young Gypsy decided to go fight in the war, on his horse, to become a big man, and to win over this girl's parents for her marriage. And so he went to the war and got himself killed. The girl cried her eyes out for days, she was very sad and couldn't believe that her darling was really dead. Some time afterwards, there was a big dance-party in the village: Gypsies made a huge fire and there were songs, food and dancing. Everybody was there and the girl came too. They all gathered around the fire, and the girl too. Suddenly, the girl noticed that her lover was there too, just that no one could see him but her. He was looking at her as if he wanted to swallow her right on the spot. The girl was scared, how come she is the only one who could see him, standing there in his military dress, looking at her and calling her name? She separated herself from her family and everybody else, and with all the courage she could gather, approached him. And he said: "Come with me, come ride with me on my horse, we'll go away!" And the girl says: "I'm coming!" They mounted his horse and galloped away, through the valleys and fields. Along the way, the boy collected some ropes and threads, all long, and the girl realized they were entering a cemetery. And she was very scared, not of him, but of graves and darkness. There was a huge gate, and the door opened by itself. The boy said: "Come, you enter first". The girl said: "No, this is your house, I don't know how to enter". So he went in first, and gave the girl all the ropes and threads, so she can make a path for where they were going. He said: "Use these, so you know how to get out in the morning and come back later on".

And this she did. They spend that night together in love, and many more afterward. Actually, what really happened was after that night at the fire, the girl fell down on her bed, sick. She was constantly repeating: "I'm not afraid, I'm not afraid". Her last words, for then she died, were: "I'm not afraid…." She is buried at the cemetery, and our people say that the boy is still looking for her….

This romantic story is very much enjoyed among the Horahane Gypsy women and girls; the recording took place in Sanela's house, a middle aged housewife, whose home was filled with her younger relatives and several older women from the settlement. We all sat on the carpet, in "Turkish style", while several of these women tried to talk all at once, elaborating on or emphasizing certain details of the story. Sanela commented: "That's how I was protected by my family too, before I got married. I got married when I was 13, for the first time. I had a baby, my son, but it didn't last. The next [marriage] lasted, but my husband would not go around looking for me, like that poor boy [in the story], he would find another woman immediately! That's how they are…" The storyteller, Sanela's cross-cousin, explained: "It's hard for our women. They have to conform to their families, then their in-laws, their men…but it's still much better to get a husband than to end up without one. They endured [in the story] in their love, and that's how we are raised to be". The emphasis on love and the enjoyment these women derive from this story does not, for the most time, concur with their own life histories. In their group/tribe, most marriages are still arranged at an early age for girls, and most have little or no say in the matter, at least not for the first marriage.

The next story, "*Pogačica*", was collected among the Gurbeti Gypsies. *Pogača* or *pogačica* is a peasant, home-made type of bread, popular in the Serbian rural areas, and made of white flour and soda bicarbonate in place of yeast. The storyteller, an aged Gypsy grandmother, introduced her story by commenting on the great significance of the topic of marriage: "Everybody has to have a marriage. That's how God wants, and parents too". Then, she turned to her fourteen year old granddaughter, pointing her finger at her and said: "Listen, you little one, listen to this, you have to get married!"

Pogačica

Once upon a time there lived in a Gypsy village a husband and wife and they had a daughter. The daughter had reached marriageable age but she wasn't married. She was twenty years old, too old by our Gypsy standards. She did not want to attend dancing parties, fairs or anything, she just sat at home. She even dressed like a man, to disguise her beauty. Then, one day, the father told the mother: "Get ready, tomorrow there is a fair in our village, make a roast chicken and let her [the daughter] make a *pogača*, and take your daughter over there, to the fair, to meet someone and get married, I've have had enough of this shame! But be sure to drink water from that small well along the road." And that is what the woman, his wife, did: she made a whole roast chicken, and the girl made *pogača* with her own hands, for she was a good cook. And they placed the food into a big scarf. And so when the new day had dawned, they, the mother and daughter, with the chicken and *pogača*, started to walk toward the fair in the village. What could they do, they had to obey. On the way there, they stopped near the well to drink some water, for they were thirsty, and as the father had instructed them. There was only one isolated house near by. The girl became hungry and started to break *pogača*, but it dropped right out of her hands and rolled and rolled until it ended up in the nearby house. The mother was angry: "What did you do, what we will offer now, at the fair? What will your father say and do? Go and get *pogača* back, you silly!" But the house was strange, there was no door, only one entrance, and the girl managed, somehow, to enter through that opening. As soon as she entered, the opening closed completely, leaving the mother outside and the girl inside. The mother started to run around, trying to find a way to get in, but nothing. And then her daughter yelled that the house is empty: "Mother, there's no one here, just this house and me, but the house is full of food, wine, water, everything is so nice and tidy. There is a room that is locked, I don't know what's inside, but I'll stay here for a while." And the mother, what she could do, she returned to her husband. This house belonged to a big, wealthy Gypsy man who was a *dzambas* [horse trader]. He was at the fair and when he returned home, he saw *pogača* in his house - sitting right there, on the ground, as if it was made for him to eat. "How has *pogaca* ended up in my house, for I have no wife of my own to make it", he asked himself aloud. Male clothes were scattered all over the room. The girl was asleep, and had taken her clothes off, but she woke up after he had spoken these words. The two looked at each others' eyes and the man thought: if she has made *pogača*, and if it is good and tasty, I will marry her, for she's beautiful and she will be a good mother and good to my family. The girl kneeled down and kissed his hand. The man said: "There is a dead man in the locked room. You have to watch over him for the next forty days, to keep flies out of his face and to wash the body. Prove that you can do it, and I will legally marry you." The girl was scared to death, but she did as he said. She went into that room, and saw the dead body. There were flies all over. And she chased off those flies for days and nights, all forty days, even though she was scared. After that period, the wealthy man kept his word, for the girl had proven she is a good cook, a good person and fearless. And that's how they become husband and wife: they went to the girl's parents and had a nice wedding. The father was very pleased, since he had known where to send his daughter. They all ate and drank, the girl was happy with her husband, and that's how the story ends.

Another woman commented:

> I could have told you this story. I lived just like that. I married late. I was a woman not a girl. My father didn't want to give me just to somebody; he waited and waited until the right man came along. My father was an important man and respected, and he wanted someone with money for me. This was my husband. He was a blacksmith, too. I married him, and that was my first and last marriage; and it was registered too. That is because my father was such a good and nice man, and he chose for me a man from a good friend's family. My father chose my husband for me; and it was a good choice.

This story bears many references to Gypsy customs surrounding marriage and confirms the importance of such unions in Gypsy culture. Food offerings, bread making and deference, and a girl wearing a man's clothes during a wedding ceremony are all customs practiced by many Gypsies in the past (Djordjević 1932:62-63). There is a saying that when a girl knows how to make bread then she can get married - she is at the right age. Food offerings substitute for dowry in the story, while the wedding story at the girl's parents' house suggests that it was paid for. The father in the story somehow "knew" that his daughter would meet "the right one" if she followed his advice, and he had directed her towards that "right one". She had to prove her courage and values and had succeeded in this. Arranged marriages are today still practiced by many Gypsy families, many Gypsy fathers claiming that not only do their girls get a "safe"/secure husband in this way, but that they extend their kinship line and future mutual obligations.

Some stories deal with mixing and intermarriage with Serbs. The following song has been sung over many generations among the Gurbeti in Mačvanski Pričinovići. An elderly male informant, Dragan Jovanović, or grandpa Dragan, as he prefers to be called, gave a brilliant performance singing and playing the song on a violin for the recording. He claimed that he learned the song from his grandfather, who had learned it from his father, and so on, because, he explained, "the song is one truly sad song."

The words to this folk song are presented along with my English translation (Čvorović 2006):

Verica i Bora	Verica i Bora
Bila jednom devojčica mala	Once upon a time there was a little Gypsy girl
Po imenu Verica se zvala	People called her Verica
Tanka, niska, nije ni visoka	That was her name.

Bistar pogled iz dva crna oka
Gde god Vera na igranku bila
Svud je Vera pobedu nosila
Visinom je kolo nadvisila
Lepotom je kola sačinila

Thin and short she was, not very tall
With a tender look from her two dark eyes.
Whenever Verica went to the ball
She was the most beautiful of all
Whenever she danced with her beauty
She made the ball.

Kad joj beše šesnaest godinica
Zaljubi se Vera za jedinca
Za jedinca, za svoga komšiju
Za nekog Boru što imade zemljicu
Al je Bora uživao slavno
Sa Vericom tri meseca ravno
Kupio joj uz nakite skupe
U ljubavi najlepše da stupe

When she was sweet sixteen
She was promised to the only son
To the only son of her [Serbian] neighbors,
To some Bora, the land owner.
Oh, how Bora enjoyed Verica
Gloriously for three months
Rich jewelry he bought her
In pleasurable love with her to enter

Kad je mesec četvrti nastao
Bora Veri ljubav otkazao
I da ne bi gubio priliku
On isprosi Miru mirazinku

When the fourth month came
Bora denied his love to Verica
And not to waste any chance
He got engaged with Mira with the dowry

I kada je nastao taj mesec peti
Jedna Vera trudna se oseti
Petnaest dana skrojila mišljenje
Dok donela konačno rešenje
Revolver je Vera pripremila
U orman ga lepo zavila

And when the fifth month came
Very pregnant poor Faith felt
For fifteen days she cut out her thoughts
Until she reached the final thought.
Then the gun was prepared by Verica
She hid it in the filing cabinet.

Kad je bilo uoči Nedelje
Kad se Bora sprema na veselje
I devojke kad mu venac viju
Ode Vera Bori na kapiju
I šetala, suze proljevala
I kroz suze Boru dozivala
Trči Bora Veri na kapiju
Luda Vero kud se dockan skitaš
I šta imaš ti mene da pitaš
Nemam Boro ništa da te pitam
Već sam došla svadbu da čestitam
I ponela sve darove tvoje
Što kod mene pet meseci stoje

When the night before the Sunday came
When Bora was ready to celebrate
When the girls have made him a wreath
To his gate Verica went
And there she cried her eyes
Through her tears she screamed his name.
Angry Bora runs to his gates:
Crazy Verica, where do you go this late?
And why do you ask for me?
Nothing, Bora, is what I ask of you
But I came to congratulate on your wedding
And I brought back all the gifts you gave me
That I have kept for five months.

Turi Vera ruke u džepove
Da izvadi Borine darove
Ne izvadi iz džepova ruka
Već revolver od petnaestog puka
Vide Bora šta će s'njime biti
I šta šta će se sa njim dogoditi

Verica put her hands in her pockets
To take out Bora's presents
No gift went out from her pocket
But the fifteenth squad revolver.
Bora saw what would be
And what will happen to him

Stade Bora u kas već da bega
A tri metka sustigoše njega
Pade Bora mrtav u avliji
Bora pade a Vera dodade
Nemoj Boro žaliti na sreću
Ja ću mlada pokraj tebe leći

Bora runs as in a trotting race
But three bullets caught him
That was his fate.
Bora fell dead in his yard
He fell and Verica says:
Don't be sorry over your happiness
I will lie, my youth, next to you

Zagrlila ga Vera oko vrata
Ko no seja svog rodjenoga brata
Zagrli ga oko vrata Vera trže
Nogu od svog revolvera
Revolver je kombinovan bio
Sve metke u Veru sručio

Verica embraced him around his neck
Like a sister with her true brother
Verica held him on his neck
She pulled the trigger of her own gun.
The revolver was ready to shoot
All the bullets in Faith it put

Od verne te jake pucnjave
Borini se u kući prestrave
Borina je majka istrčala
Sina Boru mrtvoga je ugledala

When that noisy shooting came
Bora's parents horrified became
Bora's mother ran outside to the yard
She saw dead Bora lying on the ground:

Sine Boro zar to može biti
I sa tobom se takvo dogoditi
Mesto sutra ja vesela biti
I ja se moram u mrko zaviti
Mesto sutra da stojiš uz mladu
A ti sine u zemljicu mladu
Dok su žrtvi na put stajali
Al se začu jedan glasić mali
Glasić mali Veri u stomaku
On proklinje svog oca i majku
Da ste prokleti moj otac i mati
Sve zbog vaše nesloge u ljubavi
Da ja mladjan trulim u stomaku

My son, Bora, what happened to you
Is this true, is this true?
Instead of being merry tomorrow
I will have to mourn in black and be gloomy
Tomorrow you should have stood beside your bride
Instead you will go into the ground
While people gathered around their bodies
They heard a tiny voice crying
A tiny voice from Verica's womb
Who cursed his father and his mother too:
Damn you, my father and my mother!
All because of your discord in love
I have to rot in my mother's womb.

To je bila spokojnica Vera	This was a story about lovely Gypsy Verica,
Što pogibe od svoga revolvera.	Who was killed by her own hand.

My informants told me that this song had been among the Gypsies for generations, though it is always performed in the Serbian language. In spite of the fact that much of its rhyme, rhythm, and wit are lost in translation, its sense of black humor, so characteristic of the Gypsy outlook on life, remains intact. Most of the younger informants characterized the song as belonging to their grandfathers' time, but stated that the song is beautiful and "true to Gypsies". Although there has been some intermarriage with Serbs, these Gypsies have remained largely endogamous. Grandpa Dragan, the performer declared that it is actually a "true" song, a status supported by the main character's name, Verica, which derives from the Serbian word for "faith." Whether the narrated events have a historical basis, or if the song simply reflects how Gypsies perceive the likely outcome of romantic and sexual involvement with outsiders such as Serbs, is impossible to determine. In many stories, Gypsies end up being hurt or offended in various ways by others, regardless of their own behavior or intentions. This song serves as a warning as to what might happen if one tries to undermine the Gypsy practice of endogamous marriage. Their traditional, endogamous arranged marriages appear as a more reliable and predictable option than that of marrying outside one's own group, especially in regard to the females. Even in cases of marital breakup, a relatively common occurrence among Gypsies, a woman of any age is likely to remarry, relying on her kinship group for support and guidance (Vukanović 1983, Čvorović 2004).

For my informants, the song's historical status was unimportant; the important factor was that the song comes from their ancestors and is thus "true." The unwritten rules governing marriage practice are thus seen as the word of the ancestors (see Middleton 1960:27).

Many Gypsies perceive Serbs as having intentions that are not "serious" – they complain that, in reality, Serbian males "just want to have fun" with their girls. One female informant made the case: "a Serb would never marry a Gypsy girl; even if he wants so, his family would never accept the poor girl." Actually, the attitude seems to be reciprocal; most of my informants say they will gladly trade with Serbs and do other "business" with them but would never "give away" a Gypsy girl to a Serb, unless he is "very, very rich".

For centuries, all across Europe and especially in Eastern Europe, Gypsy marriage practice patterns have remained much the same (Mirga and Mruz 1997). Endogamous mate selection, customarily based on arranged union/marriage, is the central tenet of the practice, with emphasis placed on the girl's virginity and encouragement of reproduction for all females. Females are regarded as having special importance, for they are the reproductively scarce resource, and should they "marry out," their reproductive capacity is lost to the group. In past Gypsy culture, acceptable marriage choices were largely restricted and females, in particular, were expected to marry within their tribe. These norms are met by most marriages even today, my informants explaining that the tradition of early marriage is derived from the argument that a Gypsy girl must be a virgin:

> We marry young; girls used to be married at twelve to thirteen years of age, for fourteen was considered too old, for it was assumed that she had sinned [engaged in sexual intercourse] by that age. So that's why fathers have to look upon their daughters closely: so that the girls don't fall by the wayside.

In this song, Verica broke the traditional rule of marriage endogamy: she fell for an outsider, engaged in sexual intercourse without being properly married, and became pregnant. Her punishment comes from the breakdown of tradition: abandoned by her unfaithful lover for a more suitable mate, disgraced by an out-of-wedlock pregnancy, she chose to put an end to both her own life and that of her lover. Verica's "forbidden fruit", that is, the tragic love relationship, transmits the important message: breaking with tradition can only end in tragedy.

Among the Gurbeti, endogamy is justified by the fact that girls from other Gypsy groups would not know about the particular occupational requirement specific for each group and, therefore, be useless in a family's economy:

> We used to marry only our Gypsies [endogamously]. I know why we did that: a girl who is taught to make baskets is no good for a man who makes spoons, or if she is from a Čergari group, she doesn't know anything, and can't marry a blacksmith, she would be no good to him. The same is for peasants [Serbs]: their girls know how to attend the cattle and they know agriculture, but what would they be doing married to a Gypsy who doesn't have anything? Besides, they [Serbian females] never wanted a Gypsy husband anyway.

It has always been difficult for any Gypsy, male or female, to marry into the *gadje*, in this case, a Serbian family. Despised by the Serbs, and at the bottom of every social and economic ladder, Gypsies had little chance of entering a mixed marriage.

Their story tells us as much about the Gypsy' present traditions as about their past, and many of Gypsy traditional behaviors are thus better understood. In Mačva, many have abandoned the characteristic Gypsy dress, language, nomadism and religion (Islam) but have retained their pronatalist tradition and social separation from non-Gypsies. Early endogamous marriages, encouraged fertility, and the partially imposed social segregation surely must have enabled them to survive, leave descendants and retain their ethnic identity during centuries of discrimination and poverty.

Heroine stories

In Gypsy stories, the marriage theme/finding an appropriate mate appears ubiquitous regardless of the story types, consistent with the cross-cultural patterns of characterization in folktales (Gottschall et al. 2003). Marriage is a human universal, appearing in all known cultures (Daly and Wilson 1983) but not everyone gets married. Competition in finding and securing a suitable mate can be intense, especially so among males, and the evidence suggests that human males have gained access to females primarily through marriage. Before modern times, for the bulk of the humanity, marriage was not so much an alliance between two people but an alliance between families. In many traditional societies marriages are arranged by elders, and they function as a child-rearing, economic and political institution between the spouses and among larger kinship networks (Symons 1979:122).

In Gypsy folklore many of the main characters confront the challenge of finding suitable mates, and the stories contain abundant information regarding the appropriate behavior toward this and the values typical of the Gypsy tradition. Gypsy heroine stories are no exception; in a reversal of the pattern and ways of their male counterparts (Gottschall et al. 2005), they compete for mates against life's obstacles, revealing what women want and what they are prepared to do to get it. Gypsy heroine stories are classified as a separate type by virtue of several characteristics: usually, Gypsy heroine stories are much longer and more complex than stories of the other types, and their narration requires experienced storytellers who are able to relate these stories with great precision over a couple of hours. From my experience, the storytellers are almost exclusively women. Both male and female audiences and the storytellers themselves regard these as "serious" stories, not to be taken as lightly as many others. In fact, these stories lack the typical Gypsy black humor which colors most of their stories and they lack the usual, almost direct "instructions" for behavior. The heroine stories do not simply provide examples of appropriate behavior but, owing to their dramatic tone and tragic events they describe, provide an emotionally-charged simulation of experience. During storytelling, experiencing these simulations enable the audience both to experience the emotions described and to stand back from them, allowing thus the ability to asses their own and the behavior of protagonists (Carroll 2001, Steadman and Palmer 1997).

Gottschall et al. (2005:86) argued that in folktales cross-culturally "heroines are not merely heroes with some different body parts;...there is a distinct scarcity of female characters that are heroic....". The Gypsy heroines are truly heroic, their destiny following a path of supreme dignity and suffering, while the stories place great emphasis on their courage, endurance and virtue. There are several local variants of heroine stories in every Gypsy tribe, certain details and challenges remaining the same. The Gypsies refer to this type of story as their "Cinderella". These stories center around beautiful, courageous young women, portrayed as fertile and virtuous, who are presented with various life troubles and challenges on the path to finding an appropriate mate for marriage. Presented bellow are two that best represent the story group. These two stories were collected among the Čergari and Njamci Gypsies. Both stories were told by aged grandmothers, respected within their families and the wider Gypsy community. Both storytellers are regarded as "knowledgeable" persons in Gypsy affairs, their knowledge coming from their long life and accumulated experience. In addition, both stories contain counter-stereotypes as an antithesis to many typical features and characters found in Gypsy stories. In both stories, beautiful, young, reproductively aged Gypsy women are the main protagonists, their beauty and youthfulness being connected to the central focus of the stories - marriage. Both protagonists were unmarried at the beginning of their stories and both end up, after many trials, happily married to persons of social status and wealth. Both heroines are characterized by a kind of "moral heroism", expressed in their actions and ability to endure suffering.

The following is a story told by a seventy-five year-old Čergari woman, Leposava (Čvorović 2006). Leposava grew up immersed in Gypsy traditions. She lived in the traditional Gypsy way for many years: she traveled in a *čerga* a good deal as a child. According to her, storytelling has always been important as a crucial way of obtaining knowledge among Gypsies. Today, she considers it important to make a record of "her story" for her grandchildren and younger people: Leposava refers to her story as a "cultural document". She credits her long life to the fact that her life was "just as it should be".

Gypsy Cinderella

I heard this story from my father, so it must be an old one. I used to tell this story to my children and grandchildren when they were just little kids. It's about a girl and a young emperor. This is a good one: kids learn a lot from it. Once upon a time, there was a young Gypsy girl who had two brothers.
She was really a beauty, and good in school. The best pupil. She was so clever and bright, that she soon surpassed her schoolteacher. She was more literate than he was. The schoolteacher liked her a lot, and wanted to take advantage of her—to sleep with her. He tried many times, but the girl resisted, for she was an honest creature. When he finally got tired of trying, he got angry with her, so he went to the girl's father. Her family was the richest in the county, and her father was a big man, a Roma, with status and horses and everything. So, the schoolteacher came to the house and was offered food and coffee, but he said no.

He said, "I didn't come for your food or coffee but to tell you about your daughter's debauchery." And the schoolteacher told the girl's father that his daughter is a dishonest and promiscuous woman. Her father was devastated and distraught to have heard something like that about his only daughter; he trusted the schoolteacher for this fellow was respected by the people [Serbs] in the village: he was, after all, educated and literate.

So, the father told his sons to take their sister to the woods and slay her as punishment for disgracing her family. The two brothers were very sad, but they had to obey their father's order. They took her to the place where there is no sound, no human hand, no rooster to sing or a voice to hear. A dog followed them along. They traveled for two days and two nights. When they arrived in a dense forest the brothers said, "It is a great sin to kill our sister. We will place her high on one tree with three branches, build three posts around it, and put three branches around the tree to protect her from wild animals. And we will slay the dog, and take his heart to our father." That's what they said, and that's what they did. The forest where the brothers left the girl was an [Roma] emperor's forest where he hunted every day. After three days, the emperor came to the forest to hunt; his dogs smelled the girl's flesh and started to bark at the tree where she was hiding. And the emperor said "If you are a wild animal I will shoot you. If you are not, come out and show your face." And the girl said, "My master, I am no wild animal, I am a human being." He then took her down from the tree and asked her what she was up to. She responded that she had left her village to find a job. The emperor asked her what she knew how to do and she said, "I know how to clean, and cook, and how to serve." So he decided to take the girl to his palace. So she became a servant in his palace; she was hardworking and honest, and everybody liked her.

In time, the young emperor decided to get married. He wanted a woman who could fit into his mother's shoes. He took his mother's shoe and said that a girl who can wear this shoe will be his bride. He tried and tried, went everywhere around his empire, but none of the girls could fit into the shoe. He came back home. One day, he said that the new servant should try the shoe, too, which she did, and it fitted her perfectly. The emperor's mother was furious and told him that it would be the greatest disgrace for all of them if he married an ordinary servant. The emperor stood by his decision and married the servant.

In the first year of their marriage the girl bore him one son. In their second year, a second son, and in the third year, she gave him their third son. This way she got three empires. The emperor was delighted, and out of his great love for his wife, he made her a golden swing. After their children had grown up a little, the emperor asked his wife if she had a family. "Yes," she responded, "but they live far and away, and there is no need to look for them anyway." However, he decided it was time for her to get together with her family again, now that she had three sons, and gave her an army and a major, the commander, to accompany her during her journey home. So they started to travel, the girl, her three sons, the major, and the army. They traveled day and night until they finally reached a valley where they made the camp for the night. Her tent was in the middle, surrounded by the army. Later that night, the major entered her tent and asked her in front of her children, "Will you make love to me? If not, I will slaughter your son." And she responded, "I will not have anything to do with you, ever, kill my son." And she was an empress, dressed in rich clothes, with epaulets. But the major killed her son. The next day they continued their journey; they traveled all night and day and by nightfall they had reached another valley. Her tent was in the middle, surrounded by the army. And the major entered her tent and asked again, "Will you sleep with me? If not, I will kill your second son." This time, she responded: "I will. But first I'll go outside to see if it is raining or there are stars in the sky." She went outside and ran away as fast as she could. She met some people who were shepherds and asked them to exchange their clothes with hers, and they did. She put their clothes on and gave them her nice dresses. In the morning she reached a roadhouse where her father used to drink coffee. She saw him, her father, and she stood in one corner watching him. So, he was there and he asked her, "What is with you, you good-for-nothing bump? What are you looking for?" She replied, "I came to serve here. I know horses, and how to attend them, and how to keep them and feed them." He asked, "Where will you sleep?" And she said she could sleep in the stables with the horses. She was afraid that her brothers would recognize her. Her father agreed and took her home. Three years went by. During those three years, the emperor became seriously ill. It was a nervous breakdown. Near the emperor's palace, there was a little house where an old, wise woman lived. The emperor went to see her, and she asked: "My precious emperor, what pain brings you to me?" The emperor said, "I don't have my wife anymore. I don't know where she is. I don't know where my sons are. What advice can you give me?" The old woman told him, "My advice to you is to go to every kingdom, and when people gather around you because you are an emperor, ask everybody to tell a story. That's how you will find her traces." And so he did. He went everywhere. He finally reached the village of the girl's father. People gathered around him, to eat and drink, including the schoolteacher and the major. The emperor was sweating, and he said, "I do not want food and drink, I just want that you people tell me a story." So they did. The emperor heard a lot of different stories and these went on and on. But he wasn't satisfied. Finally he asked, "Is there anybody else that can tell me a story?" And the people said, "Yes, there is one servant; he sleeps in the stables, but he is stinky and bad, and you do not want him to tell you a story." But the emperor insisted. So they brought the servant, he was dirty and smelly, and had on poor, ripped clothes. And the servant said, "My master, I will tell you a story. But you have to order to lock all doors and gates and close all windows. And light a fire in the hearth." And they did what she asked. They put locks on every door, closed all windows and lit a fire. And the servant began his story: "Do you see that man? He had one daughter. One day a schoolteacher came to him and slandered his daughter, saying that she is bad girl and that she sleeps around. And the father believed him. And her two brothers, these men over here, took her to the woods to slay her, and to bring her heart back to the father. But they killed the dog, and let her live. Then an emperor came to the forest and noticed the girl. He took her to his palace and married her. During the next three years she gave him three sons, and therefore three empires. Tell me, my master, how would you recognize your wife? And the emperor responded, "By the moon on her back and the sun on her chest." And the servant took the dirty clothes off, and there was the moon on her back and the sun on her chest. And the emperor ordered that the schoolteacher and the major be thrown into the fire. And so they burned until nothing was left of them. After that she returned to her empire. And the moon and the sun were on her.

This story describes how Gypsies see themselves - as a minority under the subjugation of the majority Serb population. On one hand, the beginning and end of the story contain an interpretation of the world and social relations with others as experienced by Gypsies. On the other hand, the story incorporates elements of other well-known folktales. In this sense, the story is a mixture of folktale and reality: it describes items such as schools and Serbian aggression and provides vivid portraits of cultural and ethnic conflict. The story incorporates many variants of familiar international folktale motifs and tale-types, especially in the extended middle section. In the beginning of the story we find the girl, the heroine, but not her brothers, enrolled in school, a counter-stereotype in which she is portrayed as very bright, diligent and chaste. In reality, many Gypsy children have low school attendance and many parents are indifferent to this fact. (Ringold 2001). By educating his only daughter, the girl's father is making a larger investment in her future: in reality, Gypsies often invest more in their daughters since females have a better chance of marrying up the socio-economic scale, thereby securing more surviving children (Bereczkei and Dunbar 1997). The heroine's husband's search for the right story represents a quest not just for an object or spouse, as in many other quest tales (for example, AT 400, man on a quest for his wife), but for the truth—the right way, the true person, a true Gypsy, and truth for Gypsies in general. Throughout the story, the motif of truth and being truthful is constantly repeated: the Gypsy heroine stays true to her own tradition and family, her chastity, and her husband, in spite of the great sacrifices she has to endure. The emperor is searching for her, that is, for the truth, and when he finally reaches it in the form of a story, everything reverts to normal, to the way it should be. In the end, the evil ones who harm Gypsies are punished and the Gypsies return to their jovial life.

The story reveals how Gypsies have mixed with non-Gypsies and the consequences suffered by Gypsies in these encounters. The underlying message appears to be that outsiders are not to be trusted since they may take advantage of Gypsies. Gypsies, as a counter-stereotype, are described as being moral, honest, and innocent victims. This counter-stereotype, though ethnocentric in some ways, illustrates the caution Gypsies have developed based on bitter experience. I have often heard Gypsies complaining that "whatever we do, it's not good enough for the peasants."

The next Gypsy heroine appears in the narrative told by Mrs. Nikolić from the Njamci Gypsies. The story is regarded as "a Gypsy original", unique to this tribe/group. The story, however, clearly illustrates how Gypsy culture and traditions have mixed with non-Gypsy cultures. "This is a horrible story" says Mrs. Nikolić, "this is how it goes, how I heard it from my mother-in-law....I was only 13 when I got married, just a child, and I enjoyed the stories very much, but this one scared me a lot!" (Čvorović 2009)

Cut, cut her hands off! or...
Gypsy Cinderella

A long time ago, one master/landlord [a Serb] used to live in this village. He had a big house, land, and a wife. It happened that his wife died; before she passed away, she said: "Here, I am leaving my husband, my house and my slippers. Whichever woman manages to wear my slippers, she'll be the one to inherit me, all of my power, possessions and status." And that's how she left this world, and her slippers. And the slippers were nice, decorated with ribbons and silk and lace. The house maid, a young Gypsy girl cleaned the house every day, and it happened that one day she found the slippers and couldn't resist trying them on, that is how pretty they were. When the landlord saw the Gypsy girl in his late wife's slippers, he started to yell and scream at the girl: "What did you do, you fool, you poor girl, misfortune will come now, don't you know that your late mistress said whoever can wear those slippers will inherit her and take her place!" The landlord was really upset and unhappy, for the girl was nice and had served him well, but what could he do, he had to punish the reckless girl. He ordered his servants to take the girl away and cut off her hands and take out her eyes. So, the servants took the girl to a nearby forest, to cut off her hands and blind her by taking out her eyes. However, the Gypsy girl was in a good standing with everybody, and with the servants too. Everybody loved her, for she was exceptionally polite, beautiful and bright. So she said to the servants: "We have served together in the house, you are good keepers, we ate and drank together, please don't cut off my hands! Please don't blind me, don't take my eyes out! Please, if you have to, cut off my hands but leave me my eyes, for how could I live without my eyes and my hands!" The keepers felt sorry and compassion for the poor girl so they said: "Here's a poor dog here, we'll take its eyes to the landlord instead of your's but we have to cut your hands off." And that's what they did. They took the dog's eyes and the girl's severed hands to the landlord. And they said: "Here, our master, are the girl's eyes and her hands; we did everything as you requested, and the girl is punished." The landlord said nothing. The girl without hands remained all alone in the forest. All by herself, wounded and scared. She ate only what she found on the ground: chestnuts, walnuts, grass, flowers, only what she could pick up with her mouth. For she didn't have any hands. Then she saw a perforated beech-tree and hid there to sleep. A few days went by, and the girl was all alone in the forest. Then one day, she heard a noise, a horse's stamping, and she managed to crawl out from her hiding place and saw a nice ornamented carriage. The carriage was parked in front of a garden full of apple trees, and she said: "I'm lucky, I will have apples to eat!" She entered the garden, and saw that all the apples were hanging really low, and she started to catch them with her teeth, for she didn't have hands. And so another few days went by; the girl without hands ate and slept in this garden full of apple trees. One day, a young man appeared in the garden; he was a custodian of the apple-trees and the emperor's son, a young prince. The forest and the apple trees belonged to the emperor. The prince immediately saw that someone had been eating the emperor's apples and asked out loud: "Who is it that who dares to eat in the emperor's garden, without his permission? Who left teeth marks on all of these apples? I can see that it is not a wild animal." He received no answer. The next day, he again came to check on the apple garden, and he saw that someone had eaten even more apples - there were half-eaten apples with teeth-marks lying all over the ground. He became really puzzled and asked again: "Who dares to steal and eat the emperor's apples?" The poor girl without hands didn't say a thing, she just crawled on the ground, biting the apples. And then, the prince spotted her: he saw a beautiful girl with shiny black hair but no hands! "What are you doing", he asked, "who gave you the permission to eat these apples?" The girl responded: "Oh, my brother, please don't ask me anything, don't ask me who permitted me to eat in this garden, I am so hungry." "What happened to your hands", asked the prince. And then the girl told him the whole story from the beginning: how well she served in a house for years, how she recklessly wore her late mistress' slippers and how her landlord had to punish her by cutting her hands off, and how, since then, she wanders about alone hungry and lonely. The prince felt compassion for the poor creature, and allowed her to stay in the garden. And day by day, she stayed in the garden, and he came to see her. In time, he fell in love with her. The prince brought her some food every day: some bread, some bacon, some water; and he fed her with his own hands. The prince gave the girl his golden ring, to protect her and guard her in his empire. One day he decided to tell his mother, the empress, about the poor girl. He said: "Mother, there is a beautiful girl in our garden, she ate our apples, and I bring her food every day and I feed her." The mother empress said: "I noticed that you were taking some food from our table, but tell me son, who's that girl?" The son related to his mother, the empress, the whole story about the poor Gypsy girl; how she served her masters well, how she made one mistake and how awful it is that she is being punished for her mistake. The mother became angry: "Why do you need a cripple, what good is this girl without hands, for she cannot do any job, will you provide for her and feed her for the rest of her life?" And the son answered: "Listen mother, what do you do? You have servants who prepare food for you, clean and care for you, while you just boss them around. This girl is a good girl, she has worked hard all of her life, and she was punished too harshly. I will bring her home, whether you like it or not." And he did so. He brought the girl without hands before his mother and father. The mother was furious, but what could she do, her son loves the crippled girl, so she allowed the girl to stay in their kitchen, near the hearth with ashes, which is why the girl is called Cinderella. Her job was to wash dirty laundry with ash, that's how they used to do it, in the past. The girl tried and tried to do washing but she couldn't do it. The girl spent the days with her beloved prince and the nights in the cold kitchen.

And so the winter came, cold and harsh, the stone was breaking, the snow was falling hard. The empress decided that the time had come for her son to find a bride. And so his parents organized many balls, dances and parties, to which the most beautiful girls from all over the empire were invited [At this point Mrs. Nikolic turns to her fifteen year old granddaughter, pointing a finger toward her and says: "You child, listen to this, it is your time now to go to these dances and find a husband, be careful whom you will chose"]. But the prince disliked each and every girl. For none was even similar to his dear handless-girl, his Cinderella. Finally, his sorrow made him ill. In the meantime, the girl without hands lived modestly, and tried to perform all of the duties given to her. She saw how her beloved man fell sick, and she felt sorry for him. One day she put the gold ring he gave her into a big pot with hot soup. And while the emperor's family was having lunch, the young prince found the ring in his soup. Everybody was puzzled: how did the emperor's ring get into his soup? But the young prince made had up his mind, and ordered that the girl be brought before everybody and proclaimed that he will marry the girl without hands or nobody else. The girl was embarrassed, for how could she marry a prince? She had no clean clothes and she didn't belong there. But she had to obey; and she was given nice clothes and made into a clean nice girl, like the ones from the ball. The mother was against the wedding, but she said nothing. Cinderella was very grateful and she promised her prince to bear him many children. She said: "I will give you a daughter with a star on her forehead and a son with a moon on his forehead, and all of their children will have the same signs, and they will form a new empire." And so it was. And the prince was pleased for he loved his wife very much even though she had no hands.

Then the time came when the young prince had to join the army and fight in a war that would last for seven long years. As soon as the young prince left, the girl without hands gave birth to two wonderful children: a daughter with a star on her forehead and a son with a moon on his forehead, just as she had promised. They were truly like emperor's children, with a sign on their foreheads, the most beautiful twins ever. But it wasn't their fate to remain so: the Mother Emperor hated the girl without hands and her children, for she was not a good mother-in-law. She was very devious: she substituted the new born children with a few puppies, placed the puppies in the emperor's children's cradle, and yelled at her daughter-in-law: "Look, you good for nothing poor girl without hands, you gave birth not to human children but to puppies!" And what could the poor girl do, nothing, so she remained silent. And the Mother Emperor wrote a letter to her only son: "Oh, Oh, my son, your wife without hands gave birth to dogs instead of a human child! Can't you see that this is such a shame and disgrace, a misfortune!" And her son replied: "Chase her away immediately, if you are telling the truth!" And so it was. The Mother Emperor chased away the girl with her two children, to wander around the world. She had tied a scarf around the girl's neck and put her children in it. The girl with her twins wandered around the world, managing the best she could, without her hands and with two small children....

After several years, the young prince returned from the war, victorious. He came home and asked his mother to tell him again about the girl without hands and how she gave birth to puppies. He then realized that something wasn't right. He asked his mother: "Where is my wife and where are my children?" And the mother replied: "I sent them away, just as you ordered. I tied a scarf around the girl's neck and placed her offspring there, and so they went off to wander around the world." The prince decided to search for his wife, and took his favorite horse and began to follow the girl's footsteps...

And the girl without hands, with a scarf around her neck and her two children inside, wandered around for days until she reached a lonely house at the crossroads. The house was empty but for one old woman who lived there alone. The old woman gave her supper, and fed her, and helped her with her children, for she couldn't even bath her own babies, she had no hands. The girl stayed with this old woman for some time and, after a while, the old woman saw that the girl was good and honest and sincere, and she said: "Listen my child, you have no hands. Get up really early tomorrow morning, before 4 am and go to this spring which is charmed. Place your arms in the water before the sun comes up, first one and then the other, and when you pull them out of the charmed spring, your hands will come back." And the girl did exactly as the old woman told her to do. And she came back from the charmed spring with both of her hands, grown again. When she came home, she was able, for the first time, to bath and care for her children. They remained in the house with the old woman for some time, and the girl cared for her children, the house and the old woman well. After some time, a lonely rider came to their house and asked if he could spend the night, for he was very tired. He said he had been traveling for years. And the old woman allowed him to stay for one night. The man started to ask if she saw anyone traveling with a scarf recently, but the old woman remained silent. And so he fell asleep. When dawn came, he was still sleeping, with one leg slung over the bed; the girl said: "My son, go and help your father, put his leg back to the bed so he doesn't get stiff when he wakes up." And the boy did so. Then the man slung his arm over the bed, and the girl said: "Go my daughter, put your father's arm back into bed so he is not hurting when he wakes up." And the girl obeyed. The old woman made some breakfast, and the man finally woke up. The old woman said: "Eh, my son, it's almost midday, wake up, we still have some talking to do. Who are you and where do you come from?" Now the man remained silent, sitting with his head down, saying nothing, just staring at the girl and her children. Then the woman started to talk: "Years ago, a young woman without hands and with two children came to my house, and I took them, and helped them, and then they helped me. This is your wife and these are your children, now take them to your home, where they belong." And the man said: "I recognized my wife and my children, but now she has both hands and before she had none but I still loved her." They both thanked the old woman and decided to go home: on one horse, the prince took his son, and on the other, the girl took their daughter, and after a long journey they finally reached home. When they got there, the son ordered that his mother, the Empress, be punished, torn to pieces by horses. And that the landlord who ordered the girl's punishment was fined a great deal of gold. And that is how it happened. The girl lived happily with her husband and two children for the rest of her life, and the children founded a new empire...

So, this was the story. That is how I will end up, torn to pieces, when I become totally useless. This is a disturbing story. We have no land of our own, hence this story takes place in the country where we presently reside. This is s very educational story, many young people can learn the proper way of behavior, how to act and meet life's troubles. It is our custom that a young bride must obey and respect her mother-in-law; but if she [the bride] has sinned, she must pay for her sins, the same as this Empress-mother-in-law - she was rightfully punished! It is the right thing to do- to give up your in-laws, even your parents, if they are not good to you.

This Gypsy story is yet another variant of the international "The Maiden without hands" folktale-type (AaTh/ATU 706). Today, Gypsies narrate it with alterations. The present Gypsy version strongly resembles the Serbian tale "Hadžija's daughter" (Popović 1905:64-67), although Gypsies omit the Christian elements. In addition, the story also includes some of the elements of other well-known folktales (AaTh/ATU 707, AaTh/ATU 510B, Mot. S 51, Mot. S 301, Mot. S 410). The middle part of the story presents as a variant of an ordinary folktale, made up of several segments of different though fragmented or altered tales, including the shoes motif (Mot. H 36.1. slipper test-identification by fitting of shoes) and the heroine's position as a servant, which refers to "Cinderella".

Just like the previous heroine story, this story is a mixture of realism and folktale. Unlike ordinary tales of similar type, the beginning of the story explains the Gypsy social circumstance and, again, the story describes the way Gypsies perceive their relationship with the Serbs. The plot begins with an authority figure who mutilates and harms the Gypsy heroine but in contrast with the tales of the similar type, it is not her father (or a brother), but her employer, a Serb. The incestuous motif (whether the daughter's or the father's projection) present in other stories of similar type (Dundes 1980, Popović 1905) is thus absent and substituted with the girl's aspiration to marry "up". The Gypsy heroine's ability to fit into the slippers of her late mistress here signifies identification with the person and her shoes: the Gypsy girl is worthy of becoming the master's wife despite her socially inferior background, position and ethnicity.

In the present story, the Gypsy heroine attempts to solve the adaptive problems concerning marriage and pursuit of the right partner, combating at the same time the repression of an ethnic group and the hostile social environment. After numerous trials, she was able to find and apply local solutions to these adaptive problems and constraints (see Scalise Sugiyama 2003). The story portrays the Gypsy heroine as beautiful, humble, passive and obedient, consistent with the description of female heroines in other world folktales that deal with marriage as a central theme (Gottschall et al. 2003). The Gypsy story describes the process of securing the right mate, as well as the consequences of pursuing the wrong one.

The Gypsies have altered the story and have hence created a variation. It is clear why and how this variant is being produced: owing to social and environmental differences, the means and information relevant to solving adaptive problems differs from place to place producing cultural variation (Scalise Sugiyama 2003). Using their experience and knowledge of social relations acquired in their interaction with the local environment, the Gypsies altered the story to serve their own ends. The girl was a good servant to her employer until the moment she decided to put on her late mistress' slippers; and although she was able to fit the slippers and so "inherit" her late mistress, she continued to be unsuitable due to her lowly background and ethnicity. And although she was not provoked or encouraged in any way by her master, the Gypsy heroine aspired to marry her master who was of a different background, and hence broke an unwritten rule of behavior concerning the appropriate marriage guidelines for Gypsies and Serbs. A mutilated outcast, the position she found herself in, is a consequence of her own behavior. The heroine's punishment is harsh: without hands, she cannot even perform duties as a servant; she is completely debased, becoming a useless, crippled and outcast creature, whose life depends on the goodwill and mercy of another human being.

This could well allude to how the Gypsies perceive of themselves in their relations with the majority: Gypsies have always constituted an oppressed caste. Since their first appearance in the Balkans, Gypsies were enslaved, forbidden to enter churches or to intermarry with whites, and were permitted to follow only certain occupations (Hancock 1987). In Serbia, these occupations (crafts and entertainment) contributed to the economy, but Gypsies were always despised by the Serbs, isolated and considered at the bottom of the social ladder (Djordjević 1932).

Dundes (1980:218), however, suggests that cutting off of one's hands stands in opposition to "giving one's hand", as in marriage, and hence the symbolism is clear. Either way, the meaning of the story for Gypsies could well be that it signifies almost any maltreatment by an authority. By replacing an authoritative father-figure with an employer of a different background, the Gypsies have projected such relationships onto the surrounding majority, the Serbs. This part of the story unveils the adaptive obstacles that Gypsies face: despised, at best only tolerated, and never fully accepted as equals by the Serbs, especially as marriage partners, it reveals the feelings of degradation and oppression that Gypsies have encountered in their interactions with the Serbs.

After many obstacles and difficulties, the heroine's subsequent marriage to a young emperor has allowed her social transformation from servant and helpless cripple to respectable woman. Perhaps the most remarkable element in the story is the Gypsy heroine's pronounced passivity with which she accepts her unfortunate fate: mutilation, degradation, abuse and slander by her mother-in-law. For the most part, she does not try to take action, complain or change her destiny in any way. The heroine has expressed a kind of moral heroism, stoically enduring all evils. In addition, unlike other heroines of tales of a similar type, she tries to conceal her obvious physical beauty, resisting even adorning herself with nice clothes.

In the story, the Gypsy heroine's only pledge in her pursuit for security is marital loyalty and obedience, symbolized by the ring the young emperor has given to her when they first met. The emperor had tried to marry a suitable girl, but was not able to find the right one in spite of the numerous eligible young women presented to him. The Gypsy heroine remained humble and silent, and by putting the ring in his soup, reminded him of her availability, submissiveness and patient waiting. These traits are generally inculcated in young Gypsy girls before marriage (Savić 2001). Status and security for this Gypsy girl could only be acquired through marriage to a person of higher status - no less so than an emperor in this case - and the only thing she has to offer is her fidelity and highly manifest submissiveness as a person. Her husband, the emperor, finally recognizes these values and accepts her for what she is. A large proportion of Gypsy stories contain three common characters: a Gypsy, a Serb (usually called peasant, master or landlord) and an emperor who, according to their own words, "has no ethnicity", but is "supranational". For any Gypsy, it was always difficult to marry into the "peasants" or into any group with clear and defined ethnic boundaries; on the other hand, in the story, a marriage to a male of higher status, regardless of ethnic background, is evidently considered a proper marriage choice for Gypsy females. It is significant that the story presents him as no less than as a young emperor without ethnicity or nationality but who, as such, is willing to marry the mutilated girl. This suggests that only a person who is not nationalistic and non-jingoistic are able to accept Gypsies as they are. The heroine's passivity, and her determination not to change her behavior and appearance, could indicate that Gypsies wish to be accepted as they are, without any effort on their part to comply with the rules of behavior governing the surrounding populations. As a separate ethnic group, Gypsies have survived reliant on their own traditions - learned cultural behavior and enhanced reproduction, the aim being to achieve the effect of behavior that in the past has contributed to their replication.

The proper marriage choice is indicated by the restoration of the girl's hands – a metaphorical reference to the fact that someone appropriate has asked for and has been granted the girl's hand in marriage (Dundes 1980:218).

The girl's marriage to the emperor reveals a preference for hypergamy; for many Gypsies in Serbia, a rise in social status is only possible through an exogamous marriage (Čvorović 2006). This is also implied by the words and behavior of Mrs. Nikolić in addressing her teenage granddaughter: she interrupted the storytelling, stressing the importance of the right choice in marriage. The importance of marrying up the socio-economic scale for Gypsies is further supported by the evidence from Hungary where Gypsy women are more likely than Gypsy men to engage in exogamous marriages (as a way of marrying up), and the survival chances of the children from such marriages are better than those of children born to endogamously married Gypsy couples (Bereczkei and Dunbar 1997).

Throughout the story, the Gypsy heroine remains true to her own passive and subservient acceptance of destiny (her "gypsyness"), and to her husband in spite of the great sacrifice and trials she has to endure. When the couple finally unites, everything is the way it should be, or the way the Gypsies would like it to be. Those who harmed the Gypsy heroine are punished and she finally gets a chance to live happily. In addition, her children, the twins, the alleged ancestors of all Gypsies, create an empire only for Gypsies. The birth of twins who eventually create a new empire, and who represent the ancestors of all Gypsies, is a recurrent motif in Gypsy stories (Djordjević 1938). For the Gypsies, this particular narrative suggests that the higher one marries up the better chances there are of acceptance, survival and reproduction.

Both of these stories involving Gypsy heroines illustrate how a variant of a worldwide folktale can be modified into a specific story that provides the knowledge necessary to pursue goals or overcome obstacles in the current local environment (Scalise Sigiyama 2001). As in many other stories, we find literary/oral narrative universals at the macro- level: Gypsy adaptive problems concerning marriage and seeking the right partner, repression of an ethnic group/minority and a hostile social environment, as well as variations at the micro level: local solutions to these adaptive problems and constraints (Scalise Sugiyama 2003).

At the beginning of both stories, the Gypsy heroines are unmarried, while the stories end with their happy marriage, children and reunion with their respective husbands. The fate of the heroines is similar: both have to endure many hardships and trials and prove their worth for the happy ending - marriage - to occur. This is a recurring motif in both oral and written literature: reproductive success, marriage/sexual union and the production of successful offspring is crucial to human concerns and hence to literary works (Carroll 1995:122). The trials test the heroines' ability to sacrifice, endure emotional and physical pain, and their commitment to "gypsyness", i.e., the right way of getting on in the world. Both characters experience social transformation after their duties are fulfilled and their marriages established from powerless girls to respectable women. Also, both of the heroines married up, in the long run presumably benefiting not only themselves but their families, and vindicating the importance that Gypsies place on kinship networks and support.

The above events also mirror the real life situation and practice: many Gypsy women become fully accepted and respected as women and wives only after they have borne children. Arranged marriages are still the most prevalent way of creating unions, whether registered or not. Also, these women are expected to be considerate of their family's well-being, requiring that much of their energy be directed to promote the welfare of close kin. For many Gypsies, a woman's highest values are her reproductive capacity and submission to natal families and in-laws, that is, her tradition. Often, if a woman is unable to produce children, she is chased off and forced to return to her parents (Čvorović 2004).

The heroine Gypsy stories describe the relationship between the human universal adaptive problem: marriage - and cultural and individual variations: local solutions to the adaptive problem, allowing both the storytellers and the audience to respond to the characters and their adventures with emotions which parallel the ones we find in observing actual people in the real world. The storytellers seek to manipulate/persuade the audience while it responds to the characters but also to the personality and mannerisms of the storytellers. This social interaction is fundamental to Gypsy folklore and an indispensable device in the interpretation of Gypsy traditional narratives.

Humorous/funny stories

Funny stories are very much enjoyed by the Gypsies and they make up the largest part of my own collection. Apart from jokes and funny stories with lascivious content, many of these funny are a mix of several types and contain a mixture of realistic and fairy-tale elements. Most often, Gypsy stories of this type seek to evoke and elicit from the audience a pronounced empathy for the main character. Boyd (2004:15) has argued that humor, like play, is fundamentally social. It can be employed in various ways, in promoting oneself or in devaluating others, or as a mean of promoting cooperation. Among Gypsies, humorous stories are used to promote cooperation and reinforce their sense of solidarity "by its self-rewarding nature and by reinforcing the recognition of shared expectations" (Boyd 2004:16). Sometimes, these stories seem to discourage or punish non-cooperation or deviance; other times they appear as a means of derogating others. Usually, the tone of these stories is good-humored and comical, producing delight because the main character manages to fulfill his desires. Most often, the main character is a male Gypsy who confronts and overcomes various trials and tribulations by use of wit and cunning.

For example, as I am informed, "Roast Chicken", is a favorite funny story among the Karavlax Gypsies, and it gets retold over and over again:

> It is always the same things, everywhere. A long time ago, here lived a young handsome Gypsy. He had a beautiful, young stepmother. His father married this young and beautiful girl, and it happened. It happened that they fell passionately in love, this young man and his stepmother. It happened because it can happen. They were very much in love, but they couldn't meet in public. It was forbidden [to make love to one's step-

> mother]. So, they had to hide, they had to hide their love in the forest and in the river. This young Gypsy had to bring a roast chicken, each time, in order to meet his love. She wouldn't meet him otherwise. And the young Gypsy managed to steal a chicken from his employer, a landlord [a Serb]. And in one green forest, they met and loved each other, each time with a roast chicken too. At home, everybody ate that roast chicken, and everybody was happy, including the father - he had a great meal every day! The only one unhappy was the landlord, his chickens going missing from time to time. That is why, when you have a roast chicken, you have everything. It doesn't matter then if you have any or no money, or how your background is, nothing matters. This is why Gypsies love the most - this roast chicken, then everything is possible and everything is allowed, even your father's wife!

This particular story epitomizes the thoughts and reactions of the Gypsies to the realities of life. It is colored with typical Gypsy humor and justification of their own, sometimes ignoble, antics by which they face life and obstacles. For the majority of Gypsies in the past as well as for many today, roast chicken on a menu every day would be considered a great feast. Many of the older and middle-aged Gypsies have recollections of the times when food was unavailable. At the same time, the provisioning of food justifies its theft, while deceit and cheating are rationalized and exonerated in the name of love and care. The young Gypsy in the story wins his stepmother's love but only after she was presented with a gift - meat, to feed her family. In this way, the young man and his lover both achieved what they had wished for - love and food. Even the father of the young man, the stepmother's husband, was happy but, of course, lacked any knowledge about the source of the food. The only damaged party in the story is the young Gypsy's employer, a *gadjo*, but his dissatisfaction or the wrong he incurred are irrelevant to the Gypsies involved. In a way, this is a typical story about the relationship between male and female - women demand meat as a right for their services, otherwise they leave their husbands or make love to other men; at the same time, "women 'are meat' to men, to be hunted with bows and arrows and 'eaten' with relish if the men are successful" (Biesele 1993:188). Much as in many other cultures, the fundamental problems for Gypsies were always how to obtain enough food and women, the two sources necessary for their survival and reproduction (Daly and Wilson 1983, Symons 1979, Buss 1994). In contrast to oral traditions in many other cultures, where the embedded commentary on the nature and social ideals in the folklore is oblique or veiled (Biesele 1993:189), that within the Gypsy humorous folklore is dramatic, direct and close to practical reality, and the supporting role fulfilled by it in social and economic survival easily perceived.

This next story was told by a grandfather of seven, a retired coffee trader, who likes to spend most of his time with his grandchildren. He feels invigorated in the company of his grandchildren and likes to help out while their parents are at work. The recording took place in Draginje while the narrator was visiting his relatives (Čvorović 2008). The storytelling and recording took place in a general atmosphere which, for Gypsies, was spontaneous and natural: the little house, containing only one room was filled with smoke; also in attendance were the narrator's relatives and neighbors who, according to their own words, would not miss out on this type of social gathering. Some food and alcohol were presented while Turkish coffee was shared among all.

The main protagonists in the following story are an "Egyptian" married couple and a poor Gypsy who "sees things", and, through his "gift", manages to obtain some benefit for himself and his family.

My Džakulica [my sack-y]

Once upon a time in ancient Egypt there was a man. He wasn't rich, but he wasn't poor either, he had his cattle and his own piece of land. And he had his wife, Stana. Everyday, he used to go out in his fields, to work, attend the cattle and so on. One day, after a long day's work, he came home, and his wife said: "Oh, man, I have a great pain in my bones." And he loved his wife, he loved his wife terribly. He loved his wife more than he loved his land and cattle. And he asked her: "My wife, what should I do? Where do I go to find you medicine?" She responded: "Anywhere, just go and do something." So, he said: "I'll do anything for you." So he went around, to other villages, but couldn't find a cure. After a few days, his wife went to bed and wouldn't get up: "Oh, man, my bones hurt so much, look how they crackle." He saw for himself how she crackles, and got really worried. And, poor man, he took off all of his dirty clothes, took a bag with some cheese, bacon and onion, and went on a long journey: to find her some medicine. And she said: "Oh, man, just get me some sea foam, and I'll get better for sure." So he went to search for the sea, to scoop some foam. And he walked, and walked, and endlessly walked. All day and all night long. He slept everywhere and anywhere; at dawn, before the birds started to sing, he would get up and continue his journey. He traveled for seven days and six nights; when the seventh night fell, he came across a little house. The house belonged to Steva, a Gypsy blacksmith. The Gypsy asked him: "Hello, my friend, where do you go?" And the man replied: "Well, you know, my wife is seriously ill, I'm going to the sea, to get some sea foam for her, and then she will recover." Steva took a good look at the man, and asked him to come in, to have some food and drinks. Steva's house was poor, little, just one small room, where he lived with his wife and their eleven children. Steva asked: "Hey, my friend, do you have any idea how far is the sea?" The man replied: "I don't know, but I have to find it. It doesn't matter how far I have to travel." Steva said: "How long have you been traveling?" The man said: "I've been on the road for seven days and seven nights." Steva argued: "You have to go seven more days and seven more nights to reach the sea. But, I'll tell you something: do not go, stay here, with us, spend the night, and we'll talk when the morning comes." The man accepted as he was tired and hungry. Steva's wife set the table and they shared food. They ate together. In the morning, they had breakfast, and the Gypsy said: "Listen, my friend, do you really believe that your wife is ill?" And the man said: "I saw for my own eyes, her bones are cracking." The Gypsy said: "Com' on, bones don't crack." And the man got angry: "Don't say things like that, my brother." The Gypsy tried to calm him down: "Please don't get upset. I'm just trying to help." And then he explained. For he had knowledge on these things: he could see the past, present and future, and had knowledge of human psychology too. And the man said, still offended: "Look how you are; I'm talking to you right from my soul, and you make fun of me, and don't believe me when I say that my wife is really ill." The Gypsy said: "I know you're a good and honest man, but your wife is not sick. In fact, there's nothing wrong with her. I see it for I have special powers. I have these powers coming to me in my dreams, and just last night I saw what your problem is." The man then suggested: "If you don't believe me, come with me to my home and you'll then see for yourself, but first I have to get her medicine." The Gypsy, the blacksmith, said: "Listen, I'll go with you - but when we approach your house, you'll get into a sack. And then, when I sing, I'll tell you what you have to do, and your wife will recover, for she's not ill at all. I saw that in my dream. And I also saw in my dream that you will reward me. I have many children and they are always hungry; I have to get them some food one way or another." And the poor man, what could he do, he crossed himself with both hands and decided to trust the Gypsy. What could the poor man do, when you are in trouble, or in pain, you believe in almost anything. So he believed the Gypsy who said that he can see things, and decided to trust him. He agreed to the plan. All this happened some 1000 years ago; people were primitive, and believed in everything. And Gypsies were always good at convincing others. So, they started a journey, again seven days and seven nights, until they reached the man's house. Some 100 meters before the house, the Gypsy ordered that the man go into the sack; the man complained again: "Hey, don't be like that, go and see that my wife is ill", but the Gypsy was determined. He tied the sack and approached the gate. "Hey, master, master, let me in." No response. And the Gypsy saw lights and music coming from the house. Again: "Master, master, let me in." And he called three times. Finally, Stana came out: "What do you want, you poor Gypsy?" The Gypsy replied: "Please, let me in. I'm cold and hungry,

> I have traveled a long way." She said: "My master is not at home, I cannot let you in." The Gypsy cried again: "Please, I don't have to eat, just let me sit by your fire, I'm very cold." Nothing - she went inside. The Gypsy said: "Please, please, please! God will give you health and fortune, just let me in." Then, her lover came out of the house, and asked: "What is it, you poor wretch, what do you want?" And the Gypsy said again: "Please let me in, I'm cold and tired, I won't stay long." And the lover agreed: "Well, come in and sit by the fire." And the Gypsy sat by the fire. After a while, the wife asked: "Hey, you, are you warm enough? If you are, go, continue your journey." The Gypsy said: "Thank you, I'm much better now. But, please don't chase me off yet. I know to sing." And the lover said: "OK, then, sing for us." But the wife didn't like the idea: "No way, just get out of my house." And the Gypsy replied: "My dear, I will sing you a song, you don't have to pay me for it, you don't have to feed me, just listen." Both the wife and her lover accepted. And the Gypsy started to sing, and sang like this: "My Džakulica [my sack-y], my Džakulica, there is an axe in the corner, my Džakulica, my Džakulica, so go take the axe, and bang the mistress, my Džakulica." And the wife listened, and laughed, and laughed: "Oh, Gypsy, what a good song this is. Sing it again, sing it again!" And the Gypsy sang it again. And while he did so, he untied he sack. And suddenly, the man jumped out, took the axe and banged his wife on her head; boom, boom, he banged and banged everything, but the lover managed to escape somehow. What will be now? The man said to the Gypsy: "If you want to eat and drink, just say so. In the morning, you will choose a cow, or a bull, or whatever you want, that will be my gift to you." And that's how the story goes. At the end, everybody is satisfied: the cheated man, the clever Gypsy with a cow. And the Gypsy was right - all along.

The narrator then explained he acknowledges that he is a Gypsy but that he traces the origin of his family back to ancient Egypt.

> My grandmother told me this story. Actually this fellow Gypsy is a cross-cousin of mine; later on, he earned a lot of money, and a title, *knez* [an ancient Serbian aristocratic title], and went to live in Serbia, with his many children. This story has been in my family for generations, that's how I know about it - our history begins with stories like this one.

This story (similar to ATU 1360C) represents an atypical situation for any Gypsy in real life: he is the one who helps a non-Gypsy with his knowledge of human nature. In the story, the Gypsy is a poor craftsman, with an occupation typical of Gypsies in the past. By describing the Gypsy as possessing of a "special gift" to foresee things, the story openly ridicules non-Gypsies and their affairs. As the story continues, it becomes evident that it takes no "special gift" to assume that

Stana, the sick wife, wasn't really ill at all, but wanted her husband out of the way. The husband, a non-Gypsy, is presented as naïve and stupid, and the story suggests he was lucky enough to have met a Gypsy who would help him with his trouble. This could well represent a stereotype that Gypsies in general may hold about non-Gypsies: while, in reality, they are poor, lack property and social power, they are portrayed in the story as being superior, smarter and more cunning than non-Gypsies. Thanks to his wit, the Gypsy is rewarded with a cow at the end of the story.

The main characters in the story have Serbian names, and one a Serbian title used in 19th century, despite the fact that the story takes place in ancient Egypt. Yet Gypsies do not find this strange or peculiar at all, as one Gypsy from the audience explained:

> Our group lived in ancient Egypt, that's why the story is happening there, and you know, it must have really happened, more or less. Someone, whoever told this story first, when we came here to live, changed the [Egyptian into Serbian] names later on, so that we could connect more with the people here.

According to many early European historical sources, Gypsies themselves disseminated the legend about their supposed Egyptian origin: they represented themselves as dukes, kings and princes from Egypt (Fraser 1992:62). In the way it is related by Gypsies today, the story exemplifies the societal changes and adaptations that Gypsies have made in order to better fit in to a new environment. The narrators have changed the characters' names so that the story can be applied to the current environment and this is acknowledged by the audience. The rationalization and justification of events, deeds or norms is present in every segment of Gypsy culture, from their stories to their real life behavior and customs. In addition, it reveals that the Gypsy storytelling tradition is not an entirely closed entity, as it is influenced also by the surrounding majority culture as well as the Gypsies' own intentions of meeting the specific requirements of the local habitat/environment.

Frequently, humorous Gypsy stories involve a favorite Gypsy character who may be a mischievous trickster, a fool, or heroic figure (Larson 2000). The next funny story describes such a creature.

The narrator is Mima, an elderly man from the village of Gornja Vranjska, who fathered six children from two marriages. He sells at the local market candles that his extended family makes at home. Mima is a gifted narrator, who uses mimicry and true acting to emphasize certain important moments in the story. He claimed that he learned the story from his mother, who was "a great actress" and true "orator" (Čvorović 2008).

Oh, Butterfly, Butterfly, You Will Fly No More

Many years ago, a poor Gypsy lived with his family in a poor little house in a village; he had nine children and had neither money nor land. The family was always hungry and the children walked around naked and barefoot, even during harsh winters. And so another cold winter came, and the Gypsy decided to visit his godfather, a Serb, to ask for some food, or money, or whatever help he could get. He did so every winter, and his godfather always helped him in one way or another. The godfather lived in the same village, in its centre, and had a nice house, much land, and abundant food. He and his whole family worked on the land - they used to grow crops and keep cattle, and they always prepared a stash of corn for the winter. Thus, the Gypsy came to his godfather's house and said: "Give me, my godfather, one meter of corn; my children have nothing to eat."

But the godfather had had enough of the Gypsy's constant pleas; he had become weary of the Gypsy, and said: "Listen, this year was not good for me and my crops, I don't know if I will have enough to feed my own family; I cannot give you any more [food]." The Gypsy replied: "If things are the way you describe them, then so be it. Thank you, and goodbye." The Gypsy went out of the house and thought to himself: "I cannot go back home with my hands empty; I have to think of something to feed my hungry children." So he figured out a plan. He crept into his godfather's stables, stole the best bull, took it to a nearby forest, and hid the animal. He didn't want to take the bull to his home for he was afraid that his godfather would see it. Instead, he hid the bull, and came up with another plan. He came home and told his wife and children to go out into the village and tell everybody that he, the poor Gypsy, could foresee the future and find lost and stolen things, including animals. And they did so—they told everybody in the village about the special gift that the poor Gypsy had so miraculously acquired.

And so the poor Gypsy became a prophet and a fortune-teller; he foretold what would happen to everyone, and how to search for whatever a person was missing. In reality, he knew nothing; he was just using his imagination and his knowledge of the human psyche. He told unmarried women that they would get married soon; he told others how to find luck in love, how to get cures for illnesses, and so on. And all of this was based only on his wit and clear mind! He started to earn good money, for the people in the village (the Serbs) would always pay to hear what they wanted to hear, and the poor Gypsy - not so poor anymore - told them what they most wanted to hear! He lied and lied about many things, and the day came when his godfather paid him a visit, and said: "Hey you, my godson, you help everybody else, please help me, too; tell me where my strongest and biggest bull is?" And then the Gypsy took a pot, filled it with plain water, and put a used bullet into it; he then took some live coals from his oven and started to throw them, coal by coal, into the water. And he gave a name to each coal. And he said:

"Who stole the bull? Is it this one, is it that one?", and so on. Then when a coal popped up from the water, the Gypsy said: "This one stole your bull; it is tied to a tree in the forest."

And that is how the Gypsy "found" the lost bull. The godfather went to the forest, found his animal, and was very grateful to the Gypsy. And the godfather showed his gratitude by sending a carriage full of food and many nice things for the Gypsy's family. And he also spread the news about this poor Gypsy; he told everybody in nine surrounding villages how the Gypsy knew and saw everything. And that is how the Gypsy became known in many places. But fortune never comes alone. The emperor had also heard about the Gypsy's deeds and sent a carriage with soldiers to fetch the Gypsy, for he had lost his precious ring and badly wanted to get it back. The ring was made of gold and also had the emperor's seal on it. So the Gypsy had to obey the order and present himself before the emperor. The Gypsy was scared to death as it was one thing to lie to his villagers, but how could he lie to the emperor? If he did, he could lose his head! He tried to explain to the emperor that he was just a poor Gypsy, without knowledge of the emperor's affairs, but it didn't work - the emperor gave him a bedroom, a servant to serve as much food and drink as he wanted and requested that he find the ring. And so the Gypsy was given all this luxury and ten days in which to solve the mystery of the missing ring. The Gypsy himself had asked for those ten days, saying: "My emperor, give me more time to solve your problem. Until now I have dealt with my own fellow Gypsies and Serbs, but your affairs are totally different and they require more time!"

And when alone in his room which had silk curtains and a nice, soft bed, the Gypsy cried and anguished for the entire ten days; but it didn't help at all. Lamenting, he said: "Oh, my poor children, soon you will have no father, for this emperor will cut off my head once he learns that I'm just a charlatan! I know nothing of foretelling the future, about emperors and rings; I'm just a poor Gypsy! Oh, my poor children, what will you do without me? I have food and drink and everything, and you are by yourselves, hungry, what will I do now?" The servant who was appointed to look after the Gypsy heard him lamenting and complaining. The truth was that the servant had taken the emperor's ring and hidden it, and now he was afraid that the Gypsy might discover who the thief was. No one knew the truth about the Gypsy, that he was a liar, a cheat and a charlatan - they had all heard only good things about him. And as the servant started to fear for his own life, he approached the Gypsy, saying: "Listen, you poor Gypsy, I don't want to lose this job, it's a good one, let's make a deal. I will return the ring to you, and you won't say a word to the emperor about who stole it. Just don't mention me, and do what you will with the ring. It doesn't mean that I will become an emperor even if I have this ring; I'm doing fine the way I am, so here's the ring, and good luck!" And the Gypsy agreed.

And so the tenth day came, and the Gypsy was brought before the emperor. The emperor said: "You ate and drank because I'm merciful, so now it's time to pay me back. Where's my ring?" And the Gypsy started to sing: "O, ring, o ring, where are you?" And he started to sing and dance all over the emperor's palace, dancing into the kitchen, opening pots, searching among the plates, and bothering people, like a true Gypsy. And so he bothered people, until he became a true bore before God, the emperor and the people. He saw a lot of turkeys in the kitchen, being prepared to be roasted for the emperor's lunch, and came up with a plan. He said to himself that the emperor had a lot of turkeys, all of which were black, excepting one which was white. He trapped the white turkey and, using a piece of bread in which he had wrapped the ring, offered it to the turkey. The turkey swallowed it with pleasure. And then the emperor said: "Come on, you Gypsy, it has been ten days, where's my ring; tell me now or I will cut off your head!" The Gypsy replied: "My emperor, I know where your ring is! It has been eaten by your turkeys!" And the emperor ordered that turkeys be slaughtered until the ring was found. And they did so; they slaughtered all of thirty turkeys, one by one. And then the Gypsy said: "Stop now, I am the only one who knows where the ring is; it is right there in this white one!" And they actually found the ring in the white turkey. Thus, it was that all were very happy - the emperor with his ring, the servant and, most of all, the poor Gypsy who had managed to keep his head on his shoulders. As a reward, the emperor gave him a horse and carriage filled with rye, corn, beans, potatoes, and all the slaughtered turkeys. And the Gypsy thought to himself: "Why did I stop then, I could have had more turkeys now to take home to my hungry kids." And he started his journey back to his home, singing along the way: "Here my darling children, I come back home, and I bring you a carriage full of food; we will have enough to eat for at least three winters; oh, how clever and witty I am, lucky me, I have this clever brain that can trick anybody, including God! And thank you God for allowing all this to happen!" And the Gypsy traveled and sang until he was approached by two Serbian soldiers. One of them said: "Here comes the Gypsy who knows the future and who can foretell everything; let's make a fool of him!" And the other soldier agreed, and caught a beautiful butterfly and hid it under his cap. And he said: "Hello Gypsy, stop!" And the Gypsy saw that yet another misfortune was in store for him! They said to him: "We know that you are a good prophet and that you can foretell things, and we will give you two coins if you manage to guess what is under the cap. If not, your head will come off your shoulders! We will reward you if you are for real [a true prophet]; if not, beware!"

And the poor Gypsy, what could he do? He said: "Oh, my people, have mercy on me, I cannot do it just like that; I need some time to think." And he started singing again: "Oh, my children, my poor children, I did everything I could; I found the missing bull for my godfather, and the ring that the emperor had lost; I did everything good, my poor children, and now that this misfortune with these two scoundrels has come my way, what shall I do?" And the soldiers harried him, [saying]: "Enough, you Gypsy, what's under the cap?" "Wait," replied the Gypsy, continuously singing all the while. And he sang: "Oh, you beautiful butterfly (referring to himself), butterfly, butterfly, you have flown, but will fly no more!" And the two soldiers said: "Look, look, the Gypsy managed to tell the truth; now, that's something new!" They released the butterfly, gave the two coins to the Gypsy, and said: "Go Gypsy, feed your poor kids and live!"

And that is how the Gypsy managed to earn more money. He finally came home and settled for some three years. He and his family ate and ate until they had finished all the food and the turkeys, and again, they were left with nothing. They ate and drank, and that is how it ended. Then the Gypsy started to make some drills to sell around the area. And so he managed to earn some money – though very little - and he would buy food for his whole family. He would bring home some bacon, divide it into nine pieces, with some for himself and his wife, and they would eat this every day. Then it happened that his eldest son took his piece and went running behind their little house. And every day the same thing would happen - the boy would grab his father's share and run out behind the house. And the Gypsy decided to follow the boy to see what he was doing. And did he have a thing or two to see! He saw his son spreading bacon all over his penis. The Gypsy got very angry, took a stick and beat his son. He said: "What the hell do you think you are doing? We have nothing to eat, and you are playing with our food; shame on you, you little delinquent!" And the boy replied: "Please, my father, don't get angry with me, and don't beat me anymore. My penis will feed you one day." At that point the Gypsy got even angrier and started to hit his son even harder. And his son couldn't take it anymore, and ran away from his home. He was about fifteen years of age at the time. He was not missed at all - it is our Gypsy custom not to search for runaway kids; we have so many that we are happy when one of them leaves or runs away from home; we are happy to get rid of at least one. And time went by, day by day, year after year, and the children grew and moved away, the wife died, and the poor Gypsy was left by himself, all alone. His children didn't help him much - that's common among Gypsies as they are so poor that they have to look out for themselves. So his children didn't visit him very much. He started to travel all alone from fair to fair, to sell little things he would make. One cold winter he found himself in a big town; it was a cold night, with snow and fog, and he didn't have a place to spend the night. Along the way he saw a bistro, and thought: "I don't have very much money, but it will be enough for one brandy; I can order one drink and stay the whole night in this bistro." He counted his coins and entered the bistro. He sat in one corner, away from the other guests, and ordered his brandy, happy to be in a dry and warm place.

The mistress of the bistro served him his drink and he said to himself: "What a beautiful lady she is!" And he sat and sat, all alone.

Then the master of the bistro came in, looked around, and said to his wife: "Listen, wife, go and ask that old Gypsy if he is hungry, and what he would like to eat and drink." And she did so, but the Gypsy replied: "I thank you for your kindness, but I have eaten this morning. I'm not hungry, I am not here to eat, just to warm up a little, it is so cold outside." But the master ordered that the best dinner and wine be put in front of him, and the old Gypsy was served with roast chicken, potatoes, and red wine, and some hot bread straight from the oven. And the master said: "Look, this is all for you, eat, and I'll get you more brandy." The Gypsy couldn't believe his eyes; were they making a fool of him? But he couldn't refuse the meal as roast chicken is a favorite Gypsy meal, and so he started to eat and enjoy it. The master asked if he could join him, whether the chicken was good, and whether he needed more bread, and so on. The Gypsy replied: "How could I prevent you from sitting next to me, this is your place; come and sit wherever you like." "Where do you come from?", asked the master. The Gypsy told him. "Do you have many children?," asked the master. "Nine or ten, I cannot remember, my master," the Gypsy said. "And where are your children?" asked the master. "God only knows," replied the Gypsy, "they all went their own way, and my wife died recently, so I am all alone in this world." Then the master said: "My wife will bring you more wine." The Gypsy replied: "No, my master, this is enough, we drink wine only on holidays." "You will get anything you want, just say so; more chicken, more wine, more brandy, more bread, and some sweets," said the master. And the old Gypsy ate well until he was completely full. When he had finished eating, the master asked him: "Did you have a son who left your house when he was fifteen?" "That is correct, my master," replied the Gypsy. "I did have a son, but he left, and I have no idea what happened to him, whether he is dead or alive. You see," said the master, "I am that son of yours. I ran away after you had beaten me, and wandered the world. And I met this woman, and her father whom I served well left me his bistro, and I married his daughter, this woman, and I am doing good business.

The old man left us a house, too, and some land. Do you see, my father, it was the truth when I told you that my penis would feed us all!"

This story invokes a typical Gypsy trait to describe and represent stereotypical Gypsy behavior. It describes how the socially weak and poor Gypsy without any real skills is able to trick and outwit people who are seen as socially stronger, in authority, be it an emperor or a member of a surrounding majority. In a way, this story could be regarded as a trickster tale, emphasizing particular teaching strategies which help to build and strengthen the morale of a given ethnic group. As for so many other tricksters, the Gypsy character is neither good nor evil; he tricks, but also can be tricked. He is also a deceiver and a cunning player: he is able to turn any situation around, at times simply because he is lucky.

The Gypsy trickster is presented as a clever, mischievous man, who tries to survive the dangers and challenges of the world using trickery and deceit as a defense. Making his way through the dangerous environment of non-Gypsies, the Gypsy trickster is able to defeat and deceive them - not by his strengths and virtues but by his wit, luck and cunning. The Gypsy trickster is unable to win any direct confrontation as he is socially weak and petty in comparison with any given authority. In the story, each time the Gypsy is confronted with a real obstacle, he insipidly cries and cries, until he "gets lucky". Meanwhile, his conduct remains mulish and boring, until everybody gets tired of him and finally complies with his wishes just to get him out of the way. This is a stereotypical form of Gypsy behavior. In Serbia, it is a strategy used with great success by Gypsy beggars. In the story, the Gypsy is portrayed as understanding of human nature: it is only by knowing the nature and lifestyle of others and taking advantage of their weaknesses, faults or stupidity that the Gypsy manages to escape their control, and ultimately succeed.

The next variant of the trickster story was collected from Mr. Vasiljković, a Karavlax Gypsy, whose family claims that he is "a real artist" at telling stories. Several themes characterize both trickster stories: the Gypsies' love of freedom and individuality, acceptance of their place in the world, their ability to adapt to local conditions and, most importantly, their finely-honed skill in adapting their own culture and traditions, as and when necessary, to that of the surrounding majority (see also Cotton 1954, Gunda 1962, Kenrick and Golemanov 1967, Larson 2000, Miller 2001). In both trickster stories, the main Gypsy protagonist is seen to benefit from his ability to outwit non-Gypsies.

The narrator, a witty man himself, enjoyed telling this story, and along with the audience - his family, several neighbors and myself - burst into laughter many times, interrupting the storytelling. The clear enjoyment of this storytelling event and the accompanying laughter created a powerful social bonding that results both from sharing of expectations and experiences and from employing that sense of shared meanings.

This version of the trickster story contains a story within a story, that is, one of the favorite Gypsy funny stories, "Roast chicken" is repeated here with some modification and told as part of the main story plot.

The Gypsy Dragon

Once upon a time, long, long time ago, in a far away place, lived a dragon who constantly kidnapped and ate young girls. He always took what he wanted, food, crops, cattle, women, houses, children, so the locals decided they had to do something about it. Since the dragon snatched at random, the people decided to create some order of his demands and stealing: they made a list who was to give what and how much of whatever the dragon wanted, and whose daughter would be given away to the dragon. So, one by one, all daughters disappeared, until there was none left but the emperor's daughter. And that emperor was like every emperor, he wanted to save his child despite the fact that he had done nothing for his people's daughters. He made a proclamation which stated that whosoever manages to save his child will receive a great reward: half of the empire will be given to this man and, in addition, he could marry the emperor's daughter. The emperor would do anything, just to save his daughter. However, no man was brave enough to offer himself for this task excepting one poor Gypsy. The Gypsy on occasion worked in the fields for his godfather [a Serb] and attended his cattle, but he wasn't satisfied with his life or his job. He also made cauldrons to sell. It was a demanding job, and he did it only to survive. Plus, he stole some chickens from his godfather to feed his family; the Gypsy believed that the godfather wouldn't notice that only a few chickens were missing - he has so many, so why not? But alas... and then afterwards he wasn't in such a good relationship with his godfather. Nonetheless, he decided to apply for the task and told his godfather about it. The godfather was curious as wasn't the job he had given him good enough? But the Gypsy replied: "Yes godfather, thank you, but I am bored with my life, and this acute poverty - I don't care anymore to live like this - it's better to die." But the godfather said: "But what will happen to your family and your nine children?" The Gypsy said: "I don't care anymore, soon they will leave and abandon me, and go their own way, never to look back. That's our Gypsy way, to be travelers and to travel all the time. Maybe they will find a better place to live. All in all, I have decided and no one will stop me." He said goodbye to his family, blessed his children and went to the emperor, to apply. He didn't look back at his children, as they will never look back at him again. The emperor laughed and laughed when he saw who was applying to be savior of his precious child, but he didn't have any other choice and so agreed. He offered the Gypsy a sword, knife, an axe, or any other such cold weapon, but the Gypsy refused. The Gypsy had his secret weapon with him all along but didn't want to reveal it. And so he went onto a cliff to await the dragon's appearance. And the dragon came: huge, ugly, with a big nozzle and smelly, and it laughed at the Gypsy: "You are the one who dares to say he'll conquer me! You are just a Gypsy lowlife, you fool, get out of here before I eat you alive along with your dirty clothes!" The Gypsy saw the kind of trouble he was in, and said: "You are so much stronger than me, I'm just a poor Gypsy, but let me tell you a story, it's kind of a riddle, actually. You are so big and smart, you will surely guess it." Amused, the dragon indulged. And the Gypsy asked: "Why it is that the roast chicken is the favorite Gypsy meal of all time, in all places, everywhere?" And the dragon thought and thought about it, but could not come up with an answer. And then the Gypsy told him the story of why it is that roast chicken is the favorite Gypsy meal of all time, in all places, everywhere: "It happens everywhere - one young Gypsy man and his step-mother were very much in love. His father had married a very young woman, he had many wives before, but had chased them away and kept just this one, young and beautiful, and so there you have it, it happened because it could happen in such situations, and they started to see each other secretly, in a nearby forest, to make love and enjoy each other. They could not meet in public for their love was forbidden, but forbidden fruit...Still, there was one condition: the Gypsy was suppose to bring her a nice roast chicken every time they meet for, if not, she refused to be with him. And he did so, many times, and she received many nice chickens. And that is how they meet, many times, to make love! When you have a roast chicken, then you have everything, it doesn't matter if you have money or not, or your background, nothing matters. And that is why Gypsies everywhere love roast chickens, when you have it, then everything is allowed, even your father's wife!" The Gypsy finished the story, and the dragon started to laugh, and laugh, and laugh so loud that he was trembling and shaking, and the whole ground was trembling, for he was so big. In a moment, while he was still laughing and shaking, the dragon lost his balance...and puff, puff, he went down the cliff! And that is how the poor Gypsy killed the dragon. He didn't defeat the dragon because he was brave and skillful, he managed to trick the dragon because he was witty and foxy. That is our famous Gypsy wittiness - being able to trick! And so, the Gypsy appeared in the Emperor's castle as a victor, and he was greeted with gratitude and joy - after all, even though he was just a Gypsy, he managed to save the emperor's daughter and the empire. Now, the time had come for the emperor to fulfill his promise: the Gypsy was to marry his precious daughter. But the mother empress was strongly against it – "How dare you, the emperor, give our daughter to marry just a Gypsy with nothing and nobody?" The emperor himself wasn't pleased either, but he had given his word, in front of everybody, so what could he do? Then, he said: "If my daughter is to marry this man, a Gypsy, let him stay here with us, it's better to have one Gypsy living with us than that he takes our daughter to wander around the world, like all Gypsies do. Or, to take her to his Gypsy castle which he doesn't have, because Gypsies do not have palaces and castles, they are travelers, and they wander the Earth forever." And the emperor said to the Gypsy: "You will live here, in this part of our palace, and I will give you my daughter, and you will have whatever you want, just do not take our daughter away, to your wandering world." But, the Gypsy, as any Gypsy, looked through the window and saw a piggery, empty, dirty, and said: "There, I will live there, that is good for me." The emperor cried: "You fool, why would you want to go and live in a piggery, like a pig, here I offer you a nice bed, soft pillows, a palace and servants!" But, the Gypsy wanted only that piggery and nothing else. He lay down on the floor and enjoyed himself. The emperor and his wife started to cry and beg, how will an emperor's daughter live in a piggery; but the Gypsy didn't care at all, he couldn't care less about what they were saying. He wanted his piggery, and that was it: if the emperor's daughter wants to come and live with him in that piggery, fine, if not, he doesn't care, and thought: "At least, I can rest before I continue my wandering." However, the emperor's daughter came to live with the Gypsy in the piggery; she respected her father's word which had been given. In the morning, after they had slept, the emperor came up with an idea: he will offer a job to the Gypsy that will take him away from his newly wed wife. And he said to the Gypsy: "Here, just say what is it that you wan to do, here's the whole army, take it, and command it, go to war, learn, travel..." The emperor would do anything just to get rid of the Gypsy. And the Gypsy agreed to the job, and headed off with the army. They traveled and traveled, and finally they reached a forest. It was a huge beech tree forest, and the Gypsy thought: "What nice trees, good for making distaff sticks. I'll take some, maybe I will need it one day." And he started to cut some young branches. His soldiers were confused: what the hell was he doing, but then decided to do the same: each and every solder took one young branch until there was no forest left. And they continued their journey until they reached a river, with no bridge; what would they do now, they cannot cross water without a bridge? The Gypsy thought: "Why do I need a stick when I cannot cross the goddamned river", and he threw away his stick, and all the soldiers did the same, copying the Gypsy. And they stopped the river all together, with their sticks, and, there you go, they made a bridge! And they crossed the river and came to the other side, to the emperor. The emperor asked his army: "Tell me, please, how did it go, how was this Gypsy?" And the army said: "Wow, he is so clever and literate, we cut down a whole forest and made a bridge to cross a river, and he was the one to think of it, how to do it; he knew that there's no bridge, and that cutting the whole forest was the only solution, he manages his brains very well, for he is so good! Thanks to him, we made that bridge and crossed the river." The emperor gave him a big award, and the Gypsy's whole family gathered around him, to praise and admire him, everybody except his godfather, the Serb. The godfather told him: "You didn't deserve any of these, for I know you." And the Gypsy became sad, and went to his piggery in sorrow. In the morning, when he woke up, he saw that a road was created connecting his piggery with the emperor's palace, and on one side there were roses and on the other side violets. The Gypsy was amused, and said: "Oh, this smells so good!" The next morning, when he woke up, he saw that a huge bunch of grapes had arisen, covering his piggery; he ate and ate grapes until he was full, and then he realized that he deserved it all.

As in the previous trickster story, this version also describes the socially powerless and disadvantaged Gypsy outwitting the socially stronger emperor and Serb, as well as a dragon that may symbolize authority of any kind. Even though the Gypsy tricks, steals and lies to others, he also engenders compassion. In effect, the characters and situations draw on the recognizable motives and emotions of Gypsy stories. In the story, we find the Gypsy being dependent on his godfather of a different ethnicity, their relationship described as not equal, to the Gypsy's disadvantage. The story implies that the reason for this disadvantage is not the fact that the Gypsy has violated the relationship by stealing from his godfather, but from the perception of the Gypsies low ethnic background in general. This notion is supported when, at the end of the story, the Serbian godfather remains the only one who refuses to acknowledge the Gypsy for his good deeds. This in turn, makes the Gypsy very sad, but his satisfaction and happy ending come when he realizes that even without the support of his ethnically superior godfather, and even in spite of it, he deserves happiness just like everybody else. For the Gypsy, the route to happiness included lying, stealing, outwitting and tricking non-Gypsies, and much luck. The justification of these behaviors comes from the fact that he possessed no other tools or social skills, so he had to rely on his wit and things close at hand that he knew well. Using the same strategy spiced with a lot of humor, he tricked and defeated the horrible dragon, won over the emperor and his daughter, and so earned his piece of happiness.

This stereotype of the Gypsy character is reflected in the historical records. Upon their arrival in Europe west of the Balkans, besides presenting themselves as Egyptian kings, Gypsies also posed as Christian pilgrims under leaders holding impressive titles. This manipulation is seen as " . . . the greatest trick . . .played on western Europe in the early fifteenth century" by Gypsies, who managed to produce letters of passage from high government officials (such as King Sigmund of Hungary), thus taking advantage of the Christian piety of the age (Fraser 1992: 62–3). After a short time, Gypsies acquired a reputation as thieves, fortune-tellers and horse dealers of questionable honesty. They were ". . . great thieves, especially their women," declared a fifteenth-century German chronicle (Fraser 1992: 67). Similar portrayals of Gypsies as thieves and tricksters are found in many other sources throughout Western Europe in the subsequent centuries (MacDonald 2002). The stereotype included colorful dress, different ethnic groups, fortune tellers, beggars, musicians and other artisan occupations. The stereotype also associated Gypsies with trickery and deception: theft, lock-picking, purse-stealing, horse-thieving, spell-casting, trickery and general witchcraft. Much of the abovementioned representations of Gypsy behavior, together with an emphasis on tricking of the *gadje*, is evident in the trickster stories presented here, where it would appear to be viewed by Gypsies as socially acceptable behavior (Sutherland 1975: 30).

In these and other many Gypsy stories, the plot revolves around the relationship and differences between Gypsies and non-Gypsies. These stories describe the ways in which Gypsies perceive differences and integrate their perceptions into the basic motives of the stories. Often in the stories, the Gypsy characters, heroines, tricksters or just ordinary Gypsies seek recognition and positive affirmation of their "gypsyness" from others, without compromising their own traditions. In many ways, the stories mirror their real life situation. Even the forces of modernization have not caused the Gypsies to compromise on their freedom of movement, choices of occupation and marriage and family patterns.

Yet, on the other hand, since their first appearance in the Balkans centuries ago, the Gypsies' main concerns were survival and overcoming their obstacles which included persecution, enslavement and harassment. The inherent insecurity of their social environment has clearly helped shape their cultural traditions, including their narratives. Their traditional stories reaffirm the strong identity with their own kinship/ethnic group while, at the same time, plead loudly for recognition. The fact that Gypsies, in spite of significant life obstacles, have successfully managed to survive as a distinct ethnic group would seem to owe much to the inherent and enduring guidance of their traditional storytelling.

IV And we were there too, we ate and celebrated!

Gypsies in Serbia have no written literature, but possess a rich and varied storytelling tradition delivered by word of mouth through the generations. The Gypsy stories presented in this book bear testimony to the evolutionarily important mechanisms employed by Gypsies to make their way in the world. Gypsy stories concern many aspects of the relationship between themselves and other social groups, both in the past and the present. At the same time, the stories deal with universal adaptive problems, such as origin/ethnicity, kinship and mate acquisition (Carroll 1999:164). By applying the concepts and folk knowledge from their own culture, Gypsies have managed to provide for themselves the guidelines to overcome these problems within a particular environment. Thus it is that these stories reflect both human universals and cultural peculiarities - by utilization of localized cultural solutions to adaptive problems. During their evolutionary history, humans have faced repeated series of tasks necessary for survival and reproduction, including acquisition of food, resources, recognition, cooperation, mate choice, childrearing, defense, and so on (Scalise Sugiyama 2003:385). Adaptive problems and the development of cognitive solutions to them are constant across all cultures and human nature has evolved to be able to address these (Carroll 1999). However, humans occupy a wide range of habitats, and a solution that works in one may not be available or adaptive in another. Adaptations are expected to be receptive to environmental differences; that is, be able to adjust to local conditions (Tooby and Cosmides 1992). In this manner, psychological adaptations interact with the local environment to produce cultural differences. The expression of a given adaptive problem varies from region to region and from group to group, and the differences between the variants correspond to differences in their environments of origin, which explains why Gypsy narratives are always placed within the context of their immediate social surroundings and environment. Unlike most other stories/tales, which have no particular reference to place or time, Gypsy stories are rooted in and share a number of cultural determinants. Often, we have seen how Gypsies have adapted or altered the stories' content to fit the local environment and to serve their own needs. The characteristics of their narratives: the function, scenery, depiction and cultural variation produced by the storytellers provide Gypsies with social knowledge and information on local surroundings that, during their history, have been so central to their survival and reproduction.

Although many Gypsies in Mačva know and can narrate parts of their genealogy and local history, only a few older people enjoy respect as true storytellers. These storytellers have the skills to remember oral literature and to entertain their audience, bringing together dramatization, moral lessons and entertainment at the same time. In this way, they are the custodians of Gypsy tradition, instructing and teaching their listeners to respect Gypsy customs. Gypsy oral literature has its distinctive artistic qualities and poetic styles but, given the nature of the traditional stories, the creativity of the storytellers is restricted. Thus, the artistic quality is achieved through features of the teller's individual character and the ways in which he/she interprets the story's emotion, mood or tension. These are expressed through varying the pace of the narration, facial mimicking, gesticulation, and, at times, altering the story to emphasize certain plots or motifs, in order to influence the audience in certain ways. Over time, Gypsy storytellers altered or combined stories, to make them more acceptable to the audience or more appropriate to a given moment or social occasion. Even though its context makes the meaning of a story clear, Gypsy storytellers at times consciously overstate the meaning, provoking comment and contemplation among the audience. This interaction between performer and audience as well as the performance situation as a whole contribute to the meaning and function of the stories: the performers frequently provoke and engage the audience such that storytelling develops into a social event.

Gypsy stories often shift in style from realism to fantasy, emphasizing the importance of performance but still keeping the conventional structure of the stories in general. Almost all Gypsy stories follow a similar pattern or form. The beginning introduces the time and place, the main characters and the problem to be solved or the conflict at the core; in the heart of the story, tasks are performed, quests begin, until the problem or conflict is resolved usually to the benefit, one way or another, of the main characters. The plots are imaginative, sometimes incorporating variants of well-known international folktales and tale-types, but never more important than the Gypsy characters, which are tailored, albeit stereotypically, to invoke sympathy. The ending is usually swift and to the point, bringing about a solution appropriate to the Gypsies.

In the basic examples of Gypsy traditional stories the plots are associated with having a practical, crucial purpose for things important to Gypsy culture but also to the individual tellers. Several major themes characterize Gypsy stories: origin narratives about a particular ancestor or a founder of the group, stories about love and marriage, a heroine and humorous/funny stories. Despite the thematic variation, these stories testify to the Gypsies' individuality, their ability to adapt to local conditions and awareness of their place in the world. The stories' historical status is unimportant to Gypsies; the important aspect is that the stories come from their ancestors, thus making them "true." By retelling the same story learned from the ancestors, Mačva Gypsies create cooperative social behavior within their own group, so transmitting culturally a form of altruism along with the particular story from one generation to the next.

Mačva Gypsy origin stories, for example, provide cultural identification and denote affiliation with specific kinship groups. These stories identify a common ancestor, a founder of the particular kinship group, and serve to establish a distinctiveness toward the other Gypsy groups in Mačva. This kind of stories emphasize kinship relatedness within a group and occupational specialization from the past, which today still serve as markers of a particular group's identity. Furthermore, the ancestral stories encourage cooperative social behavior within a group and thus increase the ability of kin groups to compete with outsiders. This is especially evident in daily affairs such as during trade or contact with the other Gypsies in the area; the social separation, as encouraged by these stories, justifies the traditional endogamy and validates the inability of Gypsies to unite as an ethnic group. Over time, Gypsies have made alterations to main characters or the settings of the stories, reflecting thus the changes that they have made in real life, such as conversion to another religion, name and identity change, adoption of Serbian last names and relocation to another country. Gypsies justify these changes by the need to adjust and survive as a group in a changing social or political environment. These stories, along with rules of behavior, are transmitted culturally from one generation to the next, suggesting the adaptive relationship for the Gypsies between the ancestral stories, cultural and behavioral practices and everyday reality.

Gypsy humorous stories, on the other hand, serve to engender and generate from the audiences forgiveness and empathy for Gypsy characters and Gypsy affairs. This is aided and achieved by the plots of these stories, which are comical and good-humored. Most often, these stories present a poor, wretched Gypsy as the main character who has to overcome various troubles and dangers, sometimes only by his wit: in doing so, he finds himself in many comical situations, producing amusement and laughter because he is able to trick and outwit those who are socially stronger or who pose a danger to him. Usually, the Gypsy character is a stereotype - he is socially week and poor, without any real skills, and he tries to survive the dangers and challenges of the world by using a little cunning and deceit as a defense. Lying to non-Gypsies, stealing and outwitting the opponents, and so on, are all presented as socially acceptable forms of behavior. In the "Roast Chicken" story, the young man cheated on everybody, his true father and an employer, just to be able to make love to his stepmother. He chose the most advantageous strategy in his given situation and achieved his wish, while his deeds found justification through typical Gypsy humor and the untroubled attitude towards the wrong he had perpetrated. In other stories of this type, for example "Oh Butterfly, Butterfly, You Will Fly No More", the Gypsy character is presented as knowledgeable of the character and weaknesses of others, and by taking advantage of human nature and stupidity, he is able to escape their control and eventually be successful. These types of humorous stories encourage not only teaching strategies and certain forms of ignoble but nevertheless justifiable behavior, but their content also helps to strengthen the morale of Gypsies as a group. These humorous stories reinforce the Gypsies' sense of solidarity and support their easygoing attitude toward the world.

Regardless of the story type, marriage/finding an appropriate mate is a pervasive theme in traditional Gypsy stories. Many of the main characters face the task of finding suitable mates and the stories evince ample information concerning the most favorable behavior toward this and values typical of Gypsy culture. As the most elaborated of all types, Gypsy heroine stories present Gypsy women, as they compete for mates against life's obstacles, in a dramatic, humor-free tone. Usually told by women only, these stories, through the tragic and moving events they describe, allow the audience to respond to the female characters and their lives with strong emotion and empathy, thus providing a simulation of the experience. These stories describe the Gypsy adaptive problems concerning marriage and finding the right mate, usually in a hostile social environment, representing also thus the repression of their ethnic group. Gypsy heroines endure many trials to prove their worth towards a happy end - marriage to men of higher status. The heroines usually exhibit moral heroism, expressed in their deeds or their willingness to endure suffering, illustrating for young Gypsy women and girls the chosen behavior for best solving the adaptive problems and constraints of marriage and the correct way of succeeding in the world.

These and other Gypsy stories provide evidence of the oral devices and stratagems in which the traditional stories are used by Gypsies to manipulate and influence the social behavior of many generations of descendants. The social strategies Gypsies use - to name just a few: trading their objective ethnic identity for the preferred one, converting to another religion, name changes and alteration of the stories to fit novel environments - create the most favorable circumstances for making ends meet. Gypsy storytellers, by granting and encouraging these and other adaptable behaviors, render the storytelling open-ended and complementary to the most favorable conditions in response to novel environmental situations.

Arensberg (1937/1988:106), in reference to rural Ireland, argued: "...to understand the local past, one must first know the local present. Only then is it clear how such traditions move and how they build on their force among men". Traditional Gypsy stories remain in the form of oral culture, the stories being one of the most significant mechanisms in the preservation and constitution of generations of young people as a separate ethnic group, signifying, thus, the great efficiency and utility of the stories as a form of communication. Frequently, the stories warn about the consequences of wrong behavior, providing, at the same time, models for proper behavior and local, grassroots knowledge on how to achieve this, as well as forewarning of situations that Gypsies might encounter in their lives. Gypsy traditional stories tell as much about the Gypsy present as about the past, but, first and foremost, they describe shared experience. Culture and social structure are consequences of the social interaction of pluralities of individuals (Murdock 1972:19), and in the case of Gypsies, their kin-groups. Most Gypsies simply state that they have never followed any specific rules of behavior other than the ones they have learned from their parents at home. The following is how a male Gypsy informant explains appropriate cultural behavior:

> I don't know what "correct" behavior is for a Roma. I don't know about other Roma in this village—how could I know, and I don't care—I only know for me. I learned from my father what correct behavior is: That's my old dad's principle. My sons are the same—they have learned how to behave, how to be a good host, from me.

In many traditional societies, young people learn about proper behavior and their roles through direct imitation of old people, as they tend to spend much time with them in various contexts (Biesele and Howell 1981:97). Generally, old people are valued for their contributions and they come to serve as models for the younger generations. These traditions and, in the case of the Gypsies, their family/kinship traditions, are "a system of information, support and guidance, serving as "cultural supplements" (Hefner 1991:123) to genetic inheritance. These traditions are passed down from ancestors to succeeding generations because they tend to influence the behavior of descendants in ways that increase their inclusive fitness and, hence, the descendant-leaving success of their ancestors (Steadman and Palmer 1997:341).

All Gypsies agree that many of their stories have an educational purpose, even if they very much enjoy the narration as form of entertainment. Given the importance of elderly storytellers in Gypsy culture and the repetition of the stories, Gypsy traditional storytelling could be termed a kinship strategy, following a parental model of influencing the behavior, especially social behavior, of children and even distant descendants (Steadman and Palmer 1997, Basso 1990).

Although a universal human activity, narrative, unlike other forms of art, is highly goal-oriented: a narrator may use narrative to manipulate an audience's perception of the social and physical environment to serve his or her own fitness needs (Scalise Sugijama 2001). The question posed here is: Which behaviors, encouraged in the foregoing stories, are deemed to have helped the Gypsy ancestors survive and reproduce in the past? Or, more simply stated: Which behaviors did we find being addressed by the above-mentioned guidelines? Or even, as Coe et al. (2006:34) put it, is there any evidence that the stories really have influenced the behavior of many generations of descendants? The key to the answer is the behavior of the protagonists in the stories and the true responses of the Gypsy audience/listeners to them.

In regard to the stories, two motives permeate almost all of their contents: encouragement of finding an appropriate mate and marriage and acceptance of "Gypsy ways" (Stewart 1997) which, in the case of Serbian Gypsies, means an emphasis on their origins and their survival in relation to others. Many Gypsy stories use stereotypes to describe character and situations, reflecting especially these two motives. Gypsy narratives rely heavily on the typical features to remain recognizable and generate meaning for the audience. The instantly recognizable nature of the Gypsy stereotypes means that they are effective in producing a certain and expected reaction from the audience. Some Gypsy stereotypes are used for dramatic effect, supported by cliché in predictable situations, in order to connect the audience with the storyteller or the meanings. A considerable body of research on stereotype formation indicates that stereotypes serve individuals' in terms of organizing the social world in an understandable way (Schaller and Conway 1999:819). Social categories can take the form of stereotypes, as shared knowledge structures, indicating the action one should perform when encountering a particular category. This categorization is universal: the ethnographic data on human social systems indicates that people about the world perceive and communicate in terms of categories (Palmer et al. 1997:303). These categories can be employed to successfully divide an environment or a society into more or less distinguishable groupings. Beliefs and other shared cognitive structures, including stereotypes, emerge and change as a result of processes similar to those that influence the evolution of biological structures (Schaller and Conway 1999, Boyd and Richerson 1985). According to the evolutionary perspective, the contents of culturally shared beliefs arise as a result of pressures through which particular variants of beliefs are selected for or against. This perspective implies that successful cultural stereotypes have proven themselves more adaptive than others (Schaller and Latane 1996:67), operating through a process of successful communication to others. In biological systems, a gene is adaptive to the extent that it is linked to phenotypes or observable behavior which assists the communication of the particular gene to other organisms. For a stereotype to be adaptive, it must be linked with behavior which increases the probability that the stereotype endures in the mind of an individual and is replicated in the minds of other individuals (Schaller and Latane 1996, Schaller and Conway 1999). Some stereotypes are more pervasive than others, and some are quite accurate (Lee, Jussim and McCauley 1995). The most persistent stereotypes maintain the association of the trait to observable, confirming instances and the utility of the trait in defining a social group as distinctive from a different group (Schaller and Latane 1996:67). On the other hand, since individuals seek to accurately predict their environment, stereotypes that do not correspond to observable behaviors are not expected to endure. Behaviors represented by stereotypes must be general enough and provide information on several, easily observable behavioral characteristics. Over time, those traits that most efficiently distinguish one group from another are most likely to become stereotypic (Ford and Stangor 1992). In addition, among the many variables imposing selection pressures on stereotypes are the aspects related to contact and communication between one individual and another. In a successful communication, there must be a sender and a receiver of a message: one has to tell and the other side has to listen, and in the case of traditional stories among kin, the receivers later have to repeat the speech and so send the same message to his or her descending kin (Coe et al. 2006). It is here where the interactive function of the traits presented and the subtle manipulative behavior of communicating individuals come into play. A stereotype is likely to be successfully transmitted to others, and consequently become mutually shared, to the extent that the communication of the trait/stereotype aids the accomplishment of individual's social goals (Schaller and Conway 1999).

Gypsy storytelling is a social activity, an exchange system of meanings between teller and audience. Older Gypsies, respected for their old age, life experience and accumulated knowledge, have often used traditional stories to manipulate and influence the social behavior of many generations of descendants. Some of the Gypsy stories or described stereotypical behavior or situations must have benefited the listeners in many ways, from acquiring information useful to the pursuit of fitness to everyday simple instructions of social behavior, or they would not have endured. By repeating the same stories to their descendants in turn, the listeners potentially influence them to do the same, just as they were influenced by their elders, fulfilling thus the social aims of those who repeat the stories created originally by their ancestors

It is for this reason that the Gypsy storytelling tradition is such a powerful tool for generating, sharing and confirming not only social categories but also instructions for behavior. And no wonder, then, that so many Gypsy elders lament their fading traditions and the influence older people once had over younger, including the ability to influence and communicate acceptance of their traditions through storytelling.

Thus, in the Gypsy stories we find stereotypical Gypsy behaviors and situations - male Gypsy characters are always portrayed as poor and wretched, sometimes careless, unable to plan for the future and dependant on an authority which, for the most time, is represented by a Serbian peasant. The representation of the peasant/landlord stands in contradistinction to the Gypsy character; hence the portrayal of the peasant is mostly as a positive, hard working, land-owning individual who provides work for the poor Gypsy, or as a godfather who shares his food with the Gypsy. On occasion, however, the Serbian peasant is presented as stupid or naïve, but almost invariably it is the poor Gypsy who violates the relationship by taking small advantages. Despite the peasant being presented as sympathetic and helpful to Gypsies, it appears that the mutual relationship or gain derived never satisfies the poor Gypsy. Regardless of the physical threat that an authority might present to the poor Gypsy - a terrible dragon, a bossy emperor or an angry Serb - it is ultimately his unequal status in relation to such authoritative figure that most bothers the Gypsy. No matter how hard the Gypsy tries to work and provide for his family, he remains poor and his family hungry, whereupon he decides to use a little cunning. In this stereotypical situation, the Gypsy is presented as being able to outwit his adversary, or able to turn situations to his own advantage, using trickery, playfulness or a little lies along the way. This mirrors the real-life situation in a way that many Gypsies perceive it - after all, humans are motivated to affiliate with and be accepted by others (Baumeister and Leary 1995) either for benefit or positive self-esteem - yet, often, complaining that no matter what or how well they do it, it is never good enough for the peasants (the Serbs). Since in the stories, and as perceived by many Gypsies in real life, Gypsies are not regarded as equals regardless of their deeds, good or bad, the Gypsy male character stereotype may provide a means of justifying their behavior and hence protecting their self-esteem against the negative implications of engaging in such behavior, whether in the context of stories or in real life (Allport 1954, Tajfel and Turner 1979). In turn, such representation serves to effectively distinguish Gypsies from non-Gypsies, allowing Gypsies to divide the social world around them into categories, sustaining and reinforcing at the same time their self-segregationist practices.

The Gypsy male stereotype is, in fact, an ethnic stereotype, i.e., a generalized representation of an ethnic group, composed of what are thought to be the typical characteristics of both genders of the Gypsy ethnic group (Fraser 1992), and supported and transmitted by the Gypsies themselves. For them, it serves to divide the social world into two major categories: the "we" and the "not we" or "others". Such representation of ethnic group membership is a contemporary parallel to the sorts of coalitional group memberships that have played an important role in social life throughout human evolutionary history (Schaller et al. 2003). Throughout this history, coalitional in-groups were sources of support and safety, while encounters with out-group members (perhaps, especially, with out-group males) represented potential threats to personal welfare.

Gypsy female characters, however, stand in stark contrast to the Gypsy ethnic stereotype, being presented as a counter-stereotype to their male counterparts. Almost invariably, Gypsy female characters are presented as hard working, humble, stoic, honest and faithful, capable of great sacrifices for higher causes, and, sometimes to their own detriment, too trusting of outsiders or men. They all exhibit strength of character, dedication and loyalty despite the various tribulations they encounter - features which the male Gypsy character lacks altogether.

As social representations do not exist in isolation from each other, and these two stereotypes appear to be mutually sustaining, the question arises as to why Gypsy male and female stereotypes differ to the extent that they do. Why was it adaptive for Gypsies to maintain these particular contrary representations for males and females throughout their stories?

In many of the stories describing marriage or the search for an appropriate mate, we find that both male and female Gypsy characters aspire either to hypogamy or hypergamy (marrying "up"). Hypergamy, is the culturally widespread tendency of females to seek mates that are relatively older, wealthier or higher in social status than themselves (Daly and Wilson 1983: 296). This is so because it is adaptive for a woman to marry up the social ladder where her children would stand to gain. Hypogamy denotes the opposite occurring: a man marrying a wife of higher education or economic status than himself (Barfield 1997:255). In the Gypsy stories, female characters, especially so the heroines, are ready to endure and suffer in order to keep intact a marriage/relationship with characters such as an emperor, a prince, a non-Gypsy (a Serb) or a wealthier Gypsy, even at great personal cost (fear, losing a child, enduring physical and emotional pain, murder and suicide). In the love story that ended tragically, viz. "Spooky Love", the Gypsy girl died of an unknown cause, implying not only that her heart was broken but also that she had made the wrong choice - the man she fell in love with was poor and not of good breeding. Verica, another of the tragic characters, sought a non-Gypsy, a Serb, supposedly as a way of marrying up, but which turned out to be another wrong choice. In the story, this was because she engaged in sexual intercourse with an outsider without being properly married and had become pregnant; perhaps as a consequence, the non-Gypsy did not consider the girl as an equal marriage partner and left her for another woman. Yet, in the end, the Gypsy heroines, after many trials and tribulations, achieved their goal - they ended up happily and properly married to persons of social status and wealth. Their destinies, and ability to endure sufferings for the right cause - a proper marriage- as well as the happy end, suggest they made the right choice.

The above stories support and encourage the practice of hypergamy, proper marriage and behavior in achieving it, by presenting the female Gypsy characters not only as young and beautiful but also in complete contrast to the Gypsy ethnic stereotype, thus indicating the traits requisite for females to marry up, either within or outside of their ethnic group, and so benefit their children. These allegorical representations are supported by the studies from Hungary, where Gypsy women are more likely than Gypsy men to engage in exogamous marriages with non-Gypsy Hungarian men (Bereczkei and Dunbar 1997). These exogamous marriages have proven beneficial since the survival chances of children from such marriages are higher than those of children born to endogamously married Gypsy couples. In addition, Gypsy women marrying Hungarian men have infants with higher birth weights, lower mortality rates and a lower incidence of developmental anomalies than Gypsy women who marry endogamously (Bereczkei 1993). Furthermore, in Bulgaria, Gypsies from mixed marriages with Bulgarians generally have higher education levels than those of endogamously married Gypsies (Ringold 2001), which could be indicative of another benefit of marrying up.

The Mačva Gypsies presumably calculated that females had greater chances by marrying up, so leaving more surviving descendants, and hence attuned their stories to show their female characters in the best light, distanced from Gypsy stereotypical behavior, to be examples for young girls and women.

The stories also reveal that several Gypsy male characters have also managed to marry up; this being achieved after risky adventures and successfully completed tasks in which, for the most part, and in contrast to the examples of the female heroines, stereotypical Gypsy behavior was employed. Some married true princesses and one a peasant girl; such marriages presumably benefiting their whole families. However, these hypogamous aspirations - a Gypsy marrying a wife of higher education or economic status than himself - are not paralleled in the everyday life of Gypsies. In Serbian society, Gypsy males, being generally of lower socio-economic status than the Serbs, cannot contribute as much in economic terms to parental investment as their Serbian counterparts do, and thus have slim chances of marrying up. Farming and agricultural land, property, and breeding stock are useful resources that Serbian peasants traditionally inherit from their parents. In addition, Serb parents generally provide their children with money for completing their schooling, obtaining goods and getting married. Quite the opposite obtains for the Gypsies who usually do not have inheritable capital and assets (see Bereczkei and Dunbar 1997 for the similar Hungarian experience). Only a few have managed to become well-off, either through trade or engaging in agriculture or breeding of animals but, mostly, such enterprises are for usage by family. The majority remain poor, while the rate of unemployment among them has even increased over the past several years to that far exceeding the Serbs.

As universal features of human nature, men prefer mates who are physically attractive while women prefer mates who show good earning potential (Buss and Barnes 1986). This is so because a woman's fertility and reproductive value is more closely connected to age and health, and hence men value female beauty because it indicates relative youth and reproductive fertility. Conversely, a selective advantage is accorded females who have a preference for men who can provide the environmental and genetic investments connected with a strong capacity to earn money (Buss and Barnes 1986, Berscheid and Walster, 1974, Buss, 1985; Langhorne and Secord, 1955, Symons, 1979).

For Gypsies in a mixed marriage, not only would a person's status be elevated, but their children would acquire wider kinship ties and better cooperation with the Serbs in the village. However, given the real and perceived low social status of Gypsy males and their slim chances in society, there is no need for the Gypsies to alter the stereotype in the stories or their behavior. Indeed, maintenance of the negative cultural stereotype serves to establish a firmer boundary between them and the others, the negative representations making no difference to the Gypsies themselves given that the traditional, endogamously arranged marriage practices ensured that every male obtained a wife.

The Gypsy stories represent a mixture of reality, fable and stereotypes. In the stories, Gypsies tend to present themselves to others/the audience in whichever way they believe would incline others to value, follow and respect them and their ways. The perception that hypogamy, hypergamy or Gypsy "ways" may lead to more surviving descendants might ultimately have shaped the contents of the stories and emerging/ accompanying stereotypes.

In Serbia, mixed marriages between the Gypsies and Serbs are rare and there are no clear data on occurrences. Within Eastern Europe, the tendency among more educated Gypsies is to attempt to leave their "gypsyness" behind by marrying non-Gypsies and hiding their true identity - their children usually become completely assimilated (Barany 2001:203). This may also be the position taken by the Gypsies in Mačva. During my fieldwork in Mačva, I encountered only three cases of registered marriages, all within the same Gypsy subgroup, and two within the same family. In the first case, a Serb married a woman from the Karavlax Gypsies (the most acculturated subgroup of Gypsies) and their son married a Karavlax girl. The first couple live in the "Serbian part" of the village of Drenovac, while the younger couple live in Šabac. The third marriage was between a Karavlax Gypsy male and a Serbian woman; they also live in Šabac. Interestingly, the woman assumed the role of a typical Gypsy woman: she is a fortune teller and herb healer, claiming much success in predicting the future, healing and even exorcism. Her husband helps with her work. They have three sons who attend a local school. Jokingly, she states that she must have been drunk when she married her Gypsy husband.

Social interrelationships are fundamental to the way of life among rural Gypsies in Mačva. Here, the most distinctive Gypsy social traditions include marriage patterns and occupations. Even today, most marriages fit the old norms. Endogamy toward the peasants - the Serbs in Mačva - is self-propagated as much as it is imposed: it is difficult for any Gypsy to marry into the "peasants". In spite of the traditional encouragement of endogamy, many male Gypsies in their jokes and conversation view marriage with a peasant girl as an "achievement" and an advantage for the particular male and his family. In fact, Gypsy endogamy has helped the sons secure wives - who else would marry them? - and thereby pass on their traditions. Gypsy girls, on the other hand, are still closely chaperoned, but if the opportunity is favorable, their marriage to peasants would be tolerated: "Why would I forbid my daughter to marry into a rich, peasant house? Even if the house is not rich, the most important thing is that people [in the house] are good. In spite of everything [different ethnic background], it's wise to wish everything of the best for your daughter: I don't want her to be hungry or to work like a mule, like we do; it's much better if the family is rich", explains a Gypsy father of two teenage daughters.

All informants insisted that the most important thing about their past was that they did not mix with other Gypsy groups. The Gypsies are born into a large circle of close and distant relatives. Their extended kinship relations and family bonds play an important role in rural Gypsy settlements and persist even among the more urbanized subgroups.

A Mačva Gypsy typically identifies with the kinship subgroup he or she belongs to, and, for many, the category of "others" includes not only non-Gypsies but also other Gypsy groups. In fact, the category of "other" has greater reference to other Gypsies than Serbs. Clear social and defining boundaries in speech and behavioral practice between "others" and "us" are frequently drawn, where "others" include all other Gypsies and "us" includes the informant' kin group in his/her village or another village inhabited by the informant's native kin. These boundaries are especially evident in the Gypsies' traditional endogamy toward other Gypsy groups. It is therefore clear why endogamous marriages were encouraged and propagated for so long a time. Amongst these Gypsies, social stratification and limited marriage choices preserved the local village traditions, both in terms of marriage and occupations. This behavior found its chief manifestation and most elaborate organization in the match of marriage. The function of this behavior, in its own settings, was to preserve local/village tradition and distinctiveness. Therefore, it is highly likely that some individual Gypsy families chose particular occupations based on their contacts with peasants and transmitted these to their descendants, which ultimately had the effect of creating a local kin group/village individuality. Gypsies became more accepted and tolerated in places where their particular occupation was valued. It was perhaps the intention of local Gypsy individuals to preserve and transmit their particular occupations by eschewing mixing and marriage ties with Gypsies in other villages, especially if they were from a different group. Groups, including families and tribes, are consequences, not causes, of social behavior (Murdock 1972, Palmer, Fredrickson and Tilley 1995). The driving force behind social behavior is parental care, which, in humans especially, is strongly influenced by ancestral traditions (Palmer and Steadman 1997). Lateral social behavior is the result of parental/ancestral encouragement of offspring to favor co-descendants, closer ones being favored over more distant ones. Endogamy restricts the range of co-descendants and thus limits the lateral extension of such behavior. It also promotes the persistence of traditions. Gypsy kin group endogamy also promoted the persistence of particular traditions. The Gypsies' success in retaining their kin group identity has been, to a great extent, due to endogamy. Their endogamy has preserved and maintained the adaptive traits, such as their reproductive and subsistence strategies, access to resources, and child-rearing practice. Arranged marriages and endogamy have thus helped to secure mates and ensure continuity of tradition.

Furthermore, for the Mačva Gypsies, telling and listening to stories helps conserve and reinforce patterns of behavior that promote kinship group success, such as endogamous marriage and respect for ancestors and traditional occupations. These stories, according to the Gypsy informants, have been retold over many generations and are often repeated with few alterations from one telling to the next. The stories are told to children and teenagers to influence their behavior in specific ways. In this way, they are a parental mode of influencing the behavior, especially social behavior, of children and, potentially, even distant descendants (Steadman and Palmer 1997).

In this sense, when the Gypsies as ethnic group became endogamous on the local level, they became almost identical to tribes, whose identification is distinguished by a common ancestry. Individuals in a tribe assume membership of a set of co-descendants, and, given the regular occurrence of marriage through time within that set, the assumption must surely be true (Steadman 1992). A tribe or an "ethnic" local Gypsy group may also be culturally distinctive: their clothing and language may communicate their ancestry, and their family names often indicate their "ethnic"/local identity. Such features are used by individuals to assert genealogical distance, on the basis of which they may systematically discriminate and favor members of their own group over outsiders. Gypsy traditions, therefore, reflect present concerns and aims as well as a longstanding inherited legacy.

Wherever they are encountered, most Gypsies maintain a social separation from non-Gypsies: they tend to remain apart from the mainstream of society by traditional, ancestrally encouraged choice (Fraser 1992, Sutherland 1975, Stewart 1997, Ringold 2001, Barany 2001). In most cases, contact with non-Gypsies is restricted to specific kinds of relationship, mostly economic exploitation and manipulation for advantage. Sutherland (1975:8, 73), studying the American Gypsies, amongst other groups the Machwaya, a group of Serbian Mačva Gypsies who emigrated to U.S.A. in the 19th century, has argued that these Gypsies generally consider themselves morally superior to non-Gypsies, while yet the practices of stealing from non-Gypsies, lying, trickery and extraction are socially expected forms of behavior.

In many of the Serbian Gypsy stories, the entire relationship between Gypsy and non-Gypsy is based on these behaviors: Gypsies value their ability to obtain money, goods or food from non-Gypsies by outwitting them. It would seem that the stories justify the stereotype, but such stereotype represents in fact an exaggerated reality, at least for the Mačva Gypsies: many of these Gypsies exhibit sycophantic behavior, especially in relation to government services and the social system as a whole. Nonetheless, they are not unique in this since many of their co-citizens, fellow Serbs, exhibit the same modes of behavior, brought about and encouraged by the 60 years of communist rule (Čvorović 2004). However, in their personal contact/relationship with others, even other Gypsies, many Gypsies mostly abandon this politic as soon as they begin to perceive a person as "unimportant" or not representing an official party or institution and further personal advantage cannot be gained. The apparently negative stereotype of Gypsy behavior represented in the stories is considered by the Gypsies themselves to reflect their behavior in general, and also in relation to that which they sometimes proclaim as "It's Gypsy business".

In the former Yugoslavia compared to other European states, the apparently strong multicultural policies promoting more favorable treatment of Gypsies coupled with a lack of forceful assimilation measures (Fraser 1992, Stewart 1997) have resulted in a greater degree of tolerance of the Gypsies (Čvorović 2004, Vukanović 1983). This, in turn, has allowed Gypsies to feel unthreatened and free to go about their business. At the same time, Gypsies, especially in the rural areas, depend on a favorable surrounding social climate and their need to make themselves more acceptable to the local majority population. This attitude is evidenced by the fact that many of the Mačva Gypsies place great emphasis on cooperation with the Serbs in their village. This cooperation is based on personal recognition and social learning – the Mačva Gypsy kin groups have been living in the same relatively small villages for generations, just as their Serbian counterparts. An old Čergari woman explains the relationship with the surrounding Serb population thus:

> My father was Toma, he was a hard working and always had good relations with the Serbs. We had our coppersmithing, and the people [the Serbs] needed us just as we needed them. My father was a Roma leader, very much respected. My godfathers are Serbs, a rich family. My family was always a good one, with the most culture among the Roma. A Serbian priest was my father's very good friend; we treat them [the Serbs] with respect, as we do our guests [visiting Gypsy relatives] and always give them some food and vine.

Economically, the Gypsies have always depended on the surrounding majority (the Serbs) as they needed to sell their handicraft, exploit their artisan skills or work on Serbian fields. Accordingly, they adjusted their behavior to create the most favorable circumstances in a given environment. Moreover, the decision

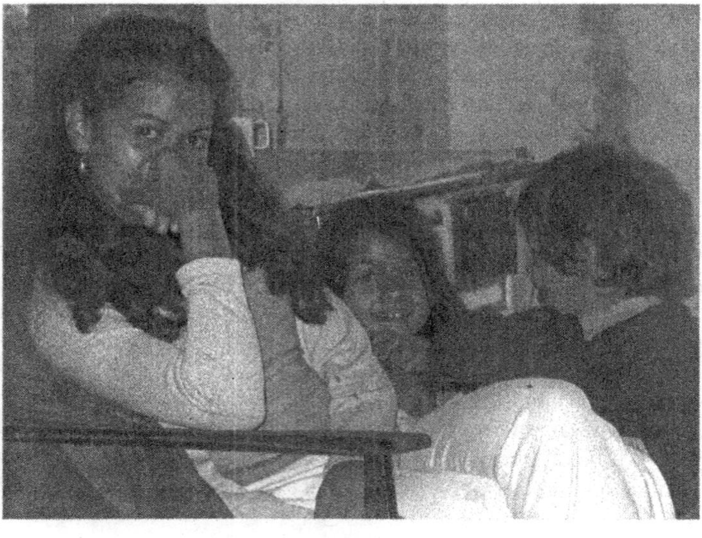

made by both parties to co-operate created mutual benefits, which in turn became the most accurate basis for predicting future interaction. The Mačva Gypsy traditional occupations made them a part of the economy, benefiting both Gypsies and non-Gypsies, and this continues today as many Gypsies play an indispensable role in the black market economy. A Gurbeti Gypsy, involved in trade and smuggling, claims that the Serbs from his village buy coffee only from him: "I lived in this same village since I was born. I never had a conflict with any peasant. The only difference between us is that they are peasants, they own and cultivate their land, and we don't do that. But they always buy goods from me, my coffee is the best in the whole Mačva, just ask anybody…"

In spite of the emphasis on cooperation with "their" peasants, most of these Gypsies have remained isolated and separate from the majority population. Most of the Serbs in rural Mačva "keep to themselves" in regard to the Gypsies, even though some of them talk about their village co-residents as "their" Gypsies. These fine social boundaries and constraints have culminated in the Mačva Gypsies receiving their "socialization" into their own little community from their ancestors. Close kin, particularly parents, are the primary socializing agents of Gypsy children. The persistence of "Gypsy socialization" in the form of traditional stories, is a sign of the strength of Gypsy traditions and of the parents' capacity to influence and "educate" their children through the generations.

The Gypsies' partial social isolation, traditional encouragement of kinship and endogamy, group differences, and traditional stories as tools for education can be seen as a kin-group evolutionary strategy. The difficult social environment has helped shape their traditions, including narrative traditions. The success Gypsies have achieved in surviving harassment, and their ability to sustain themselves and their cultures despite social rejection can be attributed, in part, to the power of the traditional stories to influence the behavior of those who hear them. For the Gypsies, telling and listening to the stories could be considered adaptive behavior: disseminating traits that were presumably successful in the past. These stories replicate and describe the environment in which the Gypsy ancestors struggled to survive. As a consequence, the narratives and the Gypsy real world are compatible in many constant and predictable ways, and many Gypsies are hence able to use narrative information/knowledge as a model for proper behavior which helps them to negotiate their social environment in their efforts to survive and reproduce. It is no surprise, therefore, that the recurring themes in their stories deal with marriage practices, other humans, non-Gypsies, and their surrounding social environment as perhaps the chief unpredictable and potentially dangerous aspects of the their past environment (Čvorović 2006, Čvorović 2008).

Generally, the stories describe the pattern of Gypsy behaviors - the widespread traits that presumably were successful in the past; in the fabled time of the stories, their life was not considered to have been much easier. Much information about the behavior, traditions and ethnicity regarding them is weaved into the artistry of the stories, to be used later as part of a general source of knowledge. The narratives so became a separating cultural mechanism, providing models of behavior with which Gypsies regulated their social and cultural surroundings, encouraging in the long run ways to reproduce such surroundings over historical time

The study of oral literature within which survival knowledge is stored, explored, reinforced and shared is central to understanding how a society maintains itself (Gottschall et al. 2005, Biesele 1993). Oral literature serves as a source of real data about human beings and their societies, and the essential communicative aspects of their cultures. Stories are the "makers" of sense of biological and social life for humans and agreement based on that sense must be reached in regard to the customs by which social activity will attain its end - the maintenance of society (Biesele 1993:47, Carroll 1995). This social agreement must be reached not once but repeatedly for each generation, incorporating new meanings and changes into the understanding of the social world. Stories thus become performances of already accepted and newly created artistic realities which produce sense both by continuity and creativity.

By maintaining their storytelling tradition, Gypsies are replicating the behavior – a particular tradition - of their ancestors who not only survived with the same behavior, but left descendants who did likewise, and, furthermore, lived to tell the story. These stories are aimed at promoting proper/successful behavior in upcoming generations, as long as there is enough similarity between the future environment and that in the past. The Gypsy "situation" has not changed much in modern times: the poor conditions of their living, low education and income and future prospects are unlikely to improve, based on their long-term past. The Gypsy "problem", their high rates of teenage pregnancy, large numbers of children, unstable pair bonds, unemployment and delinquency remain constant demographics since their arrival in Serbia (Čvorović 2004, Djordjević1932, Vukanović 1983, Stanković 1992, Save the Children. 2001, Petrović 1992, Mitrović and Zajić 1993, Mitrović 1990, Živanović 1990).

Yet, despite this, the Gypsy manipulation of isolating cultural practices has resulted in an ethnic similarity which has been immensely important in regulating their association with others. Among the Gypsies, this has probably led to a tendency to conceptualize in-group and out-groups as more homogeneous than they really are: as we have seen from the stories, the stereotypic behavior and attitudes of the in-group are positively valued, while out-group behavior and attitudes are negatively valued (MacDonald 2002, Schaller and Conway 1999).

Traditional narratives, like all traditional behaviors, can have a profoundly beneficial influence on the behavior of possibly unlimited generations of descendants of ancestors who repeated the stories previously created by their ancestors (Palmer and Steadman 1997). However, as one Gypsy concluded sadly: "We have nothing left from the olden times: our ancestors left us nothing but some stories, poverty and sorrow".

References

Abruzi, W. S. (1982). Ecological theory and ethnic differentiation among human populations. *Current Anthropology*, 23, 1, 13-24.

Adascalitei, M. (1999). *Cosmos vs. Chaos. Myth and Magic in Romanian Traditional Culture*. The Romanian Cultural Foundation Publishing House.

Allport, G.W. (1954). *The nature of prejudice*. Reading, MA: Addison-Wesley.

Anderson, B. (1996). *Imagined Communities. Reflections on the origin and Spread of Nationalism*. London. New York: Verso.

Arensberg, C. M. (1937/1988). *The Irish countryman. An anthropological study*. Prospect Height, Illinois: Waveland Press.

Arayici, A. (1998). The Gypsy minority in Europe- some considerations. *International Social Science Journal*, 156, 6, 253-262.

Barany, Z. (2001). *The East European Gypsies: Regime Change, Marginality, and Ethnopolitics*. Cambridge: Cambridge University Press.

Barfield, T. (1997). *The Dictionary of Anthropology*. Blackwell Publishing.

Barongo, E. (1997). East Africa Silent partners. UNESCO *Courier* 50, 7-8, 10-13.

Barth, F. (Ed.). (1969). Ethnic groups and boundaries. The social organization of culture difference. Boston: Little Brown.

Basso, K. (1990). *Western Apache Language and Culture: Essays in Linguistic Anthropology*. Tucson, Arizona: University of Arizona Press.

Baumeister, R. F. and Leary, M. R. (1995). The need to belong: Desire for interpersonal attachments as a fundamental human motivation. *Psychological Bulletin*, 117:497-529.

Bellman, J. (1993). *Stereotypes: The Gypsies in Literature and Popular Culture. The Style Hongrois in the Music of Western Europe*. Boston: Northeastern University Press.

Bellman, J. (1998). *The Hungarian Gypsies and the Poetics of Exclusion. The Exotic in Western Music*. Boston: Northeastern University Press.

Beischeid, E., and Walster, E. (1974). Physical attractiveness. In: L. Berkowitz (Ed.), *Advances in experimental social psychology* (pp. 157-215). New York: Academic Press.

Benjamin, W. (1973). *Illuminations*. London: Fontana Press.

Bereczkei, T. (1998). Kinship Network, Direct Childcare, and Fertility Among Hungarians and Gypsies. *Evolution and Human Behavior* 19, 283–298.

Bereczkei, T. and Dunbar, R. I.M. (1997). Female-biased reproductive strategies in a Hungarian Gypsy population. *Proc. R. Soc. Lond. B*, 264, 17-22.

Biesele, M. (1993). *Women like meat. The folklore and foraging ideology of the Kalahari Ju/'hoan*. Bloomington and Indianapolis: Witwatersrand University Press. Indiana University Press.

Biesele, M. and Howell, N. (1981). "The Old People Give You Life": Aging Among !Kung Hunter-Gatherers. In: P.T. Amoss, and S. Harrell (Eds.), *Other Ways of Growing Old: Anthropological Perspectives* (pp.77-98). Stanford University Press.

Boyd, B. (1998). Jane met Charles: Literature, evolution and human nature. *Philosophy and Literature*, 22, 1, 1-30.

Boyd, B. (2001). The origin of stories: Horton hears a who. *Philosophy and Literature,* 25, 2, 197-214.

Boyd, B. (2004). Laughter and literature: a play theory of humor. *Philosophy and Literature,* 28, 1-22.

Boyd, B. (2005). Evolutionary theories of art. In: J. Gottschall and D. S. Wilson (Eds.), *The Literary Animal* (pp. 147-176). Evanston, IL: Northwestern UP.

Boyd, R. and Richerson, P.J. (1985). *Culture and the evolutionary process*. Chicago: University of Chicago Press.

Brown. D. J. (1991). *Human Universals*. New York: McGraw-Hill.

Buss, D.M., and Barnes, M. (1986). Preferences in human mate selection. *Journal of Personality and Social Psychology*, 50, 3, 559–570.

Buss, D. M. (1985). Human mate selection. *American Scientist*, 73, 47- 51.

Čajkanovic, V. (1924). Božićna slama. *Prilozi*, 3, 123-132.

Čajkanović, V. (1973). *Mit i religija u Srba. Izabrane Studije*. Beograd: Srpska Književna zadruga.

Calame-Griaule, G. (1986). *Words of the Dogon world*. Philadelphia: Institute for the study of Human Issues.

Carroll, J. (1995). Evolution and Literary Theory. *Human Nature,* 6, 2,119-134.

Carroll, J. (1999). The Deep Structure of Literary Representations. *Evolution and Human Behavior,* 20, 159-173.

Carroll, J. (2002). Adaptationist Literary Study: An Emerging Research Program. *Style*, 36, 4, 597–617.

Carroll, J. (2001). Human universals and literary meaning: A sociobiological critique of Pride and Prejudice, Villette, O Pioneers!, Anna of the Five Towns, and Tess of the d'Urbervilles. *Interdisciplinary Literary Studies*, 2, 9-27.

Carroll, J. (2002). Organism, Environment, and Literary Representation. *Interdisciplinary Studies in Literature and Environment,* 9, 2, 27-43.

Clifford, J. (1988). *The Predicament of Culture*. Cambridge, MA: Harvard University Press.

Coe, K. (2003). *The ancestress hypothesis*. Newark: Rutgers University Press.

Coe, K., Palmer, C.T. Aiken, N., and Cassidy, C. (2005). The Role of Traditional Children's Stories in Human Evolution. *Entelechy: Mind and Culture* (fall 2005/winter 2006). www.entelecyjournal.com.

Coe, K., Aiken, N., and Palmer, C.T. (2006). Once upon a time: Ancestors and the Evolutionary Significance of Stories. *Anthropological Forum*, 16, 1, 21-40.

Cotten, R. M. (1954). Gypsy Folktales. *The Journal of American Folklore*, 67, 261–266.

Crowe, D.M. (1996). *A history of the Gypsies of Eastern Europe and Russia*. New York: St. Martin's Griffin.

Cruikshank, J. (1992). *Life lived like a story. Life stories of Three Yukon Native Elders*. The University of Nebraska: First Bison Books.

Čvorović, J. (2004). Sexual and Reproductive Strategies among Serbian Gypsies. *Population & Environment*, 25, 217–242.

Čvorović, J. (2005). Gypsy Oral History in Serbia. *Oral History Journal*, 33, 1, 57-68.

Čvorović, J. (2006). Gypsies Drown in Shallow Water: Oral Narratives among Macva Gypsies. *Journal of Folklore Research*, 43, 2, 129–48.

Čvorović, J. (2008). A Gypsy, Butterfly and Gadje: Narrative as Instruction for Behaviour. *Folklore*, 119, 1, 29-44.

Čvorović, J. Rushton, J.P. and Tenjevic, L. (2008). Maternal IQ and Child Mortality in 222 Serbian Roma (Gypsy) Women. *Personality and Individual Differences*, 44, 1604-1609.

Čvorović, J. (2009a). Losing a River: The Social Significance of Gypsy Oral Tradition. *Fabula*, 50, 2, 37-53.

Čvorović, J. (2009b). Between Preferred and True Identity. *Oral History Review*, 36, 1, 45-70.

Courthiades, M. (1999). Towards a Typology of Balkan National Communities: Non-territorial Groups. Unpublished manuscript.

Daly, M. and Wilson, M. (1983). *Sex, evolution, and behavior*. Belmont, CA: Wadsworth Publishing Company.

Daly, M. and Wilson, M. (1999). *The Truth about Cinderella: A Darwinian View of Parental Love*. New heaven: Yale University Press.

De Laguna, F. (1997). *Under Mount Saint Elias: The history and culture of the Yakutat Tlingit*. Washington, DC: Smithsonian.

Di Maggio, P. (1997). Culture and Cognition. *Annual Review of Sociology*, 23, 263-287.

Djordjević, T.R. (1924). *Iz Srbije Kneza Miloša. Stanovništvo—naselja*. Beograd: Geca Kon.

Djordjević, T.R. (1932). *Naš narodni zivot I običaji*. Knjiga VI. Beograd. Knjizevna Zadruga.

Djurić, R. (1987). *Seobe Roma*. Beograd: BIGZ.

Dundes, A. (1980). *Interpreting Folklore*. Bloomington: Indiana University Press.

Dundes, A. (1969). Comments on Jason, Heda: A Multidimensional Approach to Oral Literature. *Current Anthropology*, 10, 4, 421-422.

Elkin, A. (1964). *The Australian Aborigines*. Garden City: Doubleday.

Erlanger, S. (2000). Across a new Europe, a people deemed unfit for tolerance. *New York Times*, April 2, B1, 16.

Ford, T.E., and Stangor, C. (1992). The role of diagnosticity in stereotype formation: Perceiving group means and variances. *Journal of Personality and Social Psychology*, 63, 356-367.
Fraser, A. (1992). The Gypsies. Cambridge: Blackwell.
Gottschall, J., R. Berkey, M. Cawson, C. Drown, M. Fleischner, M. Glotzbecker, K. Kernan, T. Magnan, K. Muse, C. Ogburn, S. Patterson, C. Skeels, S. St. Joseph, S. Weeks, A. Welsh & E. Welch. (2003). Patterns of Characterization in Folktales Across Geographic Regions and Levels of Cultural Complexity. *Human Nature*, 14, 365-382.
Gottschall, J. Berkey, R., Cawson, M., Drown, C., Fleischner, M., Glotzbecker, M., Kernan, K., Magnan, T., Muse, K., Ogburn, C., Patterson, S., Skeels, C., Joseph, S., Weeks, S., Welsh, A., Welch, E. (2005). The heroine with a Thousand faces: Universal Trends in the Characterization of Female Folk Tale Protagonists. *Evolutionary Psychology*, 3, 85-103.
Gunda, B. (1962).Gypsy Medical Folklore in Hungary. *The Journal of American Folklore*, 75, 131–46.
Hancock, I. (1987). *The pariah syndrome: an account of Gypsy slavery*. Ann Arbor, MI: Karoma Publishers.
Hallowell, A. (2002). *The Ojibiwa of Berens River, Manitoba: Ethnography Into History*. Belmont, CA: Wadsworth.
Hefner, P. (1991). Myth and morality: The Love Command. *Zygon: Journal of Religion and Science,* 26, 115-136.
Hobsbawn, E. (1983). The Invention of Tradition. In E. Hobsbawn, and T. Ranger (Eds.), *The Invention of Tradition* (pp. 1-14). Cambridge: Cambridge University Press.
Jackson, B. (1997). The stories people tell. *The Antioch Review*, 55, 3, 261-267.
Kalaydjieva L, Calafell F, Jobling MA, Angelicheva D, de Knijff P, Rosser ZH, Hurles M., E, Underhill P, Tournev I, Marushiakova E, Popov V. (2001). Patterns of inter- and intra-group genetic diversity in the Vlax Roma as revealed by Y chromosome and mitochondrial DNA lineages. *European Journal of Human Genetics*, 9, 2, 97-104.
Kalaydjieva, L., Perez-Lezaun, A., Angelicheva, D., Onengut, S., Dye, D., Bosshard, N., Jordanova, A., Savov, A., Yanakiev, P., Kremensky, I., et al. (1999). A founder mutation in the GK1 gene is responsible for galactokinase deficiency in Roma (Gypsies). *American Journal of Human Genetics*, 65, 1299-1307.
Kenrick, D., and Golemanov, D. (1967). Three Gypsy Tales from the Balkans. *Folklore*, 78, 59–60.
Kuokkanen, R. (1998). Restory-ing the Sami strength. *ReVision,* 21, 1, 11-14.
Larson, J. R. (2000). *The Fish Bride and Other Gypsy Folktales*. North Haven, Conn: Linett Books.

Laederich, S. (2000). Rroma, Ashkali, Egyptians. A Kosovo Peculiarity. Rroma Foundation Reports, April 2000. www.romnews.com/kosovo.html

Lee. Y.T., Jussim, L.J., and McCauley, C.R. (1995). *Stereotype accuracy: Toward appreciating group differences.* Washington, D.C: American Psychological Association.

Liegeois, J.P. (1994). *Roma, Gypsies, Travelers.* Council of Europe. Strassbourg.

Liegeois, J. P. and Gheorghe, N. (1995). *Roma/Gypsies: A European Minority.* London: Minority Rights Group International.

Langhorne, M. C., and Secord, P. F. (1955). Variations in marital needs with age, sex, marital status, and regional composition. *Journal of Social Psychology, 41,* 19-37.

MacDonald, K. (2002). *A People That Shall Dwell Alone.* Lincoln, Neb.: Writers Club Press.

Malinowski, B. (1931). Culture. In: E.R.A. Seligman and A.S. Johnson (Eds.), *Encyclopedia of the Social Sciences* IV (pp. 634-642). New York: Macmillan Publishing Co.

Marushiakova E., and Popov, V. (1997) *Gypsies (Roma) in Bulgaria.* Frankfurt am Main: Peter Lang.

Marushiakova, E., and Popov, V. (2001). The Gypsy Minority in Bulgaria – Policy and Community Development. In: C. McDonald, J. Kovacs, and C. Fenyes (Eds.), *The Roma Education Resource Book* (pp.63-106). Budapest: Open Society Institute, Institute for Educational Policy.

Maynard-Smith, J. (1984). Science vs. myth. *Natural History,* November, 11-24.

McDonald, C., Kovacs, J., and Fenyes, C. (2001). The Roma Education Resource Book 2. Budapest: Open Society Institute, Institute for Educational Policy.

Middleton, J. (1960). *Lugbara Religion.* London: Oxford University Press.

Miller, C. (2001). Luck and Three Gypsy Folktales. *Journal of Folklore Research,* 38, 263–84.

Miller, G. (2000). The Mating Mind: How sexual choice shaped the evolution of human nature. New York: Anchor Books.

Mirga, A., and Mruz, L. (1997). *Romi, Razlike I Tolerancije.* Beograd: Akarit.

Mitrović, A. (1990). *Na dnu. Romi na granicama siromaštva.* Beograd: Naučna Knjiga.

Mitrović, A. and Zajić, A. (1993). *Decenija sa Romima u Masurici. Društvene promene I položaj Roma.* Beograd: Srpska Akademija Nauka i Umetnosti.

Murdock, G.P. (1972). Anthropology's mythology. *Proceedings of the Royal Anthropological Institute of Great Britain and Ireland* for 1971, 17-23.

Narayan, K. (1996). First sour, then sweet: Women's ritual story telling in the Himalayan foothills. *Women and Language,* 19, 1, 9-14.

Nedeljković, S. (2003).. Etno-antropološke dileme u više dimenzija: Egipćani u Beogradu. *Tradicionalno i savremeno u kulturi Srba,* posebna izdanja, EI SANU 49, 309-328.

Nedeljković, V. (2002). Svaka sličnost nije slućajna. *Iskra*, 1. maj.
Noncheva, T. (2002). *Social profile of ethnic groups in Bulgaria.* Sofia: Center for the Study of Democracy. Sofia. www.csd.bg/news/Club2EthnicB-speech.htm.
Oxfam and Belgrade Institute for Health Protection. (2003). *Roma health.* Oxfam, Great Britain and the Belgrade Office.
Palmer, C. T., Fredrickson, E., & Tilley, C. F. (1997). Categories and gatherings: Group selection and the mythology of cultural anthropology. *Evolution and Human Behavior,* 18, 291-308.
Palmer, C.T. and Steadman, L.B. (1997). Human kinship as a descendant-leaving strategy: a solution to an evolutionary puzzle. *Journal of Social and Evolutionary Systems,* 20, 1, 39-51.
Petrović, R. (1992). Demografske osobenosti Roma u Jugoslaviji. In *Razvitak Roma u Jugoslaviji: problemi I tendencije* (pp.115-127). Beograd: SANU.
Pinker, S. (1997). *How the Minds Works.* New York: Norton.
Popović, P. (1905). *Pripovetka o devojci bez ruku.* Beograd: Srpska Kraljevska Akademija.
Ringold, D. (2001). Education of the Roma in Central and Eastern Europe: Trends and Challenges. In C. McDonald, J. Kovacs and C. Fenyes (Eds.), *The Roma Education Resource Book 2* (17-42). Budapest: Open Society Institute, Institute for Educational Policy.
Save the Children (2001). *Denied A Future? The Right To Education of Roma, Gypsy and Travelers Children.* Save the Children Fund. United Kingdom.
Savić, S. (2001). *Romkinje.* Novi Sad: Futura Publikacije.
Scalise Sugiyama, M. (2001a). Food, Foragers, and Folklore: The Role of Narrative in Human Subsistence. *Evolution and Human Behavior*, 22, 4, 221–40.
Scalise Sugiyama, M. (2001b). Narrative theory and function: Why evolution matters. *Philosophy and Literature*, 25, 2, 233-250.
Scalise Sugiyama, M. (2003). Cultural variation is a part of Human Nature. *Human Nature*, 14, 4, 383-396.
Scalise Sugiyama, M. (1996). On the origins of narrative: storyteller bias as a fitness-enhancing strategy. *Human Nature*, 7, 403-425.
Schaller M., Park, J. H, and Faulkner, J. (2003). Prehistoric dangers and contemporary prejudices. *European Review of Social Psychology*, 14, 105–37.
Schaller, M. and Conway, L.G. (1999). Influence of Impression Management Goals on the Emerging Contents of Group Stereotypes: Support for a Social-Evolutionary Process. *Personality and Social Psychology Bulletin*, 25, 7, 819-833.
Schaller, M. and Latane, B. (1996). Dynamic social impact and the evolution of social representations: A natural history of stereotypes. *Journal of Communication,* 46, 4, 64-71.

Stanković, V. (1992). Romi u svetu podataka Jugoslovenske statistike. In *Razvitak Roma u Jugoslaviji: problemi I tendencije,* 159-179. Beograd:SANU.
Steadman, L.B. (1992). Kinship, religion and ethnicity. Paper presented at the annual meetings of the Human Behavior and Evolution Society, Albuquerque. NM.
Steadman, L. and Palmer, C. (1997). Myths as Instructions from Ancestors: The Example of Oedipus. *Zygon*, 32, 341–50.
Stewart, M. (1997). *The Time of the Gypsies*. CO: Westview Press.
Storey, R. (1996). Mimesis and the Human Animal: On the Biogenetic Foundations of literary Representation. Evanston, IL: Northwestern UP.
Stokes, G. (1993). The Walls Came Tumbling Down: the Collapse of Communism in *Eastern Europe*. Oxford: Oxford University Press.
Sutherland, A. (1975). *Gypsies: The Hidden Americans*. New York: The Free Press.
Symons, D. (1979). *The evolution of human sexuality*. New York: Oxford University Press.
Tajfel, H. and Turner, J. (1996). The Social Identity Theory of Intergroup Behavior. In S. Worchel and W.G. Austin (Eds.), *Psychology of Intergroup Relations* (pp.7-24). Chicago: Burnham Inc Pub.
Tong, D. (1989). *Gypsy Folktales*. Harvest Book. Harcourt Brace & Company. New York. London.
Tooby, J., and Cosmides, L. (1992). The Psychological Foundations of Culture. In: J. Barkow, L. Cosmides, and J. Tooby (Eds.), *The Adapted Mind* (pp.19-136). New York: Oxford University Press.
Uther, Hans-Jorg. (2004). *The Types of International Folktales, Parts I-III*. Helsinki: Academia Scientiarum Fennica.
Vaughn, T. (1978). *Mammalogy*. Philadelphia: Saunders College Publishing.
Vukanović, T. (1983). *Romi (Cigani) u Jugoslaviji*. Vranje: Nova Jugoslavija.
van den Berghe, P.L. 1979. *Human Family Systems. An Evolutionary View*. New York: Elsevier Press.
Wilson, E.O. (1975/2000). *Sociobiology: the New Synthesis*. Cambridge, MA: Harvard.
Zemon, R. (2001). *Balkanski Egipćani. Istina o Egipćanima sa Kosova i Metohije.* Beograd: Nacionalna zajednica Egipćana Kosova i Metohije.
Živanović, M. (1990). Romi se dave u gluvoći sveta. *Romologija,* 1, 85-88.